CCCC STUDIES IN WRITING & RHETC
Edited by Victor Villanueva, Washington

The aim of the CCCC Studies in Writing & Rhetoric Series is to influence how we think about language in action and especially how writing gets taught at the college level. The methods of studies vary from the critical to historical to linguistic to ethnographic, and their authors draw on work in various fields that inform composition—including rhetoric, communication, education, discourse analysis, psychology, cultural studies, and literature. Their focuses are similarly diverse—ranging from individual writers and teachers, to work on classrooms and communities and curricula, to analyses of the social, political, and material contexts of writing and its teaching.

SWR was one of the first scholarly book series to focus on the teaching of writing. It was established in 1980 by the Conference on College Composition and Communication (CCCC) in order to promote research in the emerging field of writing studies. As our field has grown, the research sponsored by SWR has continued to articulate the commitment of CCCC to supporting the work of writing teachers as reflective practitioners and intellectuals.

We are eager to identify influential work in writing and rhetoric as it emerges. We thus ask authors to send us project proposals that clearly situate their work in the field and show how they aim to redirect our ongoing conversations about writing and its teaching. Proposals should include an overview of the project, a brief annotated table of contents, and a sample chapter. They should not exceed 10,000 words.

To submit a proposal, please register as an author at www.editorial manager.com/nctebp. Once registered, follow the steps to submit a proposal (be sure to choose SWR Book Proposal from the drop-down list of article submission types).

TOWARD A NEW RHETORIC OF DIFFERENCE

Stephanie L. Kerschbaum
University of Delaware

Conference on College Composition and Communication

National Council of Teachers of English

Staff Editor: Bonny Graham
Series Editor: Victor Villanueva
Interior Design: Mary Rohrer
Cover Design: Mary Rohrer and Lynn Weckhorst

NCTE Stock Number: 54953

It is the policy of NCTE in its journals and other publications to provide a forum for the open discussion of ideas concerning the content and the teaching of English and the language arts. Publicity accorded to any particular point of view does not imply endorsement by the Executive Committee, the Board of Directors, or the membership at large, except in announcements of policy, where such endorsement is clearly specified.

Every effort has been made to provide current URLs and email addresses, but because of the rapidly changing nature of the Web, some sites and addresses may no longer be accessible.

Publication partially funded by a subvention grant from the Conference on College Composition and Communication of the National Council of Teachers of English.

Library of Congress Cataloging-in-Publication Data
Kerschbaum, Stephanie L., 1977-
 Toward a new rhetoric of difference / Stephanie L. Kerschbaum, University of Delaware.
  pages cm. — (CCCC studies in writing & rhetoric)
  Includes bibliographical references and index.
  ISBN 978-0-8141-5495-3 (pbk : alk. paper)
 1. English language—Rhetoric—Study and teaching (Higher)—Social aspects—United States. 2. Minority college students—United States. I. Conference on College Composition and Communication (U.S.) II. Title.
  PE1404.U6K47 2014
  808'.0420711073—dc23   2013043731

To my parents

CONTENTS

Permission Acknowledgments   ix

Acknowledgments   xi

Introduction: Rethinking Diversity in Writing Studies   1

1. The Market for Diversity in Higher Education   29

2. Marking Difference: The Emergence of Difference as an Interactional Phenomenon   56

3. Reading and Writing Difference in the Composition Classroom   79

4. Writing Risky Relationships: Marking the Limits of Difference   118

Coda: Returning to the Big Picture   150

Notes   153

Works Cited   159

Index   179

Author   187

PERMISSION ACKNOWLEDGMENTS

Elements from the introduction and Chapters 2 and 3 were previously published in a different version in "Avoiding the Difference Fixation: Identity Categories, Markers of Difference, and the Teaching of Writing." *College Composition and Communication* 63.4 (2012): 617–45.

Some material from Chapter 2 and the narrative analysis in Chapter 3 appeared in a different form in "Classroom Narratives and Ethical Responsibility: How Markers of Difference Can Inform Teaching." *Narrative Discourse Analysis for Teacher Educators: Managing Cultural Difference in Classrooms.* Ed. Lesley Rex and Mary Juzwik. Cresskill, NJ: Hampton Press, 2011. 77–104.

ACKNOWLEDGMENTS

THIS BOOK WAS SUPPORTED BY FUNDS FROM a University of Delaware General University Research Grant, a Texas A&M University Glasscock Center Fellowship, and a grant from the Wisconsin Center for the Advancement of Postsecondary Education. This project also benefited from support from the University of Delaware President's Diversity Initiative to participate in the National Center for Faculty Development and Diversity's twelve-week Faculty Boot Camp.

Many audiences provided feedback, thoughts, insight, and encouragement during the time I was working on this book, including Cheryl Ball, Michael Bernard-Donals, Lynn Bloom, Brenda Brueggemann, Jennifer Clary-Lemon, Christine Cucciarre, Alice Daer, Rasha Diab, Elias Dominguez-Barajas, Dawn Fallik, David Fleming, Cecilia Ford, Karen Gisladottir, Beth Godbee, Naomi Greyser, Jennifer Griffith, Mary Juzwik, Amy Johnson Lachuck, Ed Larkin, Rhea Lathan, Donna LeCourt, Cindy Lewiecki-Wilson, Michael McCamley, Sara Michael-Luna, Rebecca Nowacek, Martin Nystrand, Shifra Sharlin, and Tisha Turk. Thanks, too, to the fantastic audience at a talk delivered at Spelman College in March 2013 and to the participants at the 2009 Symposium for the Study of Writing and Teaching Writing at the University of Massachusetts–Amherst.

Many people engaged with drafts of my work-in-progress, especially Melissa Ianetta, who read, multiple times, just about every page of the entire manuscript, and Margaret Price and Deborah Brandt, whose feedback at critical moments kept me going. Thanks to Nadia Brown, Jay Dolmage, Jenny Dumont, Cecilia Ford, Joe Harris, Elizabeth Ho, Mary Juzwik, Jimmie Killingsworth, and Amy Vidali for their willingness to push my work in new directions. Special thanks to Juan Guerra, Ellen Cushman, and Christopher Schroeder for incisive and insightful suggestions for revision that strengthened this project immeasurably, and to Victor Villanueva and Robin Gosser, as well as Bonny Graham at NCTE, for their guidance in bringing this project to completion.

I'm incredibly fortunate to have completed this work at the University of Delaware, where many colleagues have supported my work in a variety of ways—particular thanks to Maggie Andersen, Gretchen Bauer, Stephen Bernhardt, Iain Crawford, Emily Davis, Rebecca Davis, John Ernest, Meryl Gardner, Gabrielle Foreman, Carol Henderson, Melissa Ianetta, James Jones, Heidi Kaufman, Matthew Kinservik, Robin Schulze, Regina Sims, and Miranda Wilson.

Thanks to the graduate students from my "Introduction to Composition Theory and the Teaching of Writing" course, who read and responded to a draft of Chapter 2: Kerry Hasler-Brooks, Elyse Brown, Amelia Chaney, Elizabeth Downs, Michael Harris-Peyton, Erica Jansen, Natalie James, Joana Koebsel, Ashley Sarpong, Lara Southgate, and Nicole Sweeney.

Sarah Keberlein and Deborah Pfuntner's transcription work was invaluable, and Bob Wyckoff helped manage study files and organization.

As always, a rock star shout-out to Nadia Brown, Joan Furey, and Jenny Oser.

To Dahlys Hoot, Davin Yannick, Tiffany Ballou, Heather Allman, Debbie Bakitis, Jaela Matthews, and Jessica Richards: thanks for always believing in me.

Deepest thanks to Charlie, D. C., and Yvonne, the teachers who invited me into their classrooms, and to their students, who shared their first-year writing experiences with me.

Finally, I owe much to Dick and Holly Kerschbaum, who always thought I would write a book; to Debbie and Whit Sutherland, the best in-laws I could ever ask for; and to Jamie, Rosemary, and Rhys for their love and support, which sustains me and enriches my work.

Introduction: Rethinking Diversity in Writing Studies

DURING A PILOT STUDY INTERVIEW WITH Charlie,[1] a PhD student in his first year of composition teaching at a large public midwestern university, he described his current class in terms of students who participate "fairly actively on a regular basis," students who on any given day may contribute to a discussion, and students who do not talk. After making these observations, he offered some hypotheses as to why some students are quiet in class: "I'm not sure if this is a difference, if it's just a psychological phenomenon, that some people are shy, that's why they don't participate, or if this has something to do with their own conception of themselves as thinkers or writers."[2] As we continued to talk, he parsed additional potential explanations, noting, for instance, that his more vocal students were also from large out-of-state urban cities, while many of his quieter in-state students were from small rural communities. Throughout the conversation, it was clear that Charlie cared deeply about working with his students and that he was eager to learn ways to reach those students he worried he was not reaching.

I have had many conversations like this one with teachers about their classrooms. In such talk, differences are frequently called out as singular or unusual, but they are not always examined alongside the (sometimes unstated or assumed) norms against which those differences are often cast. Why do these observations about everyday teacher talk matter for the teaching of writing? First, they matter because how teachers orient to students affects teacher–student relationships as well as students' learning. Second, as a burgeoning ethnographic literature on students and student writing reveals, there is much that teachers don't know or don't understand about their students (see, e.g., Chiseri-Strater; Fishman and McCarthy; Herrington and Curtis). Such ethnographic research has immeasurably enriched our field's knowledge and helped many teachers more effectively reach populations that have been underserved or misunderstood. Given that how teachers understand difference matters to the way they teach writing,[3] how might Charlie work through his questions about reaching quiet students? One place to start is, of course, with the observations he has already made. But it is not enough for Charlie to conjecture that students' geographic origins might correlate with their classroom presence. His tentative explanations need to be put in conversation with other resources that can help him develop those hypotheses without relying on stereotypes or idiosyncratic experiences. As Charlie put it during our interview:

> You ask the question why do certain people talk and why other people don't talk and then give an analysis based on differences in either gender or racial differences, class differences; I have a student who feels enfranchised to speak and who doesn't. And that's a really helpful analysis, but then on a certain level when you're in the classroom it becomes very personalized. You know that some of the generalizations, for example, that males will participate more often in classroom discussions than females definitely hold true in the classroom. They seem to hold true, right, [but] they don't always hold true.

Charlie wants to avoid orienting to his students by focusing on stereotypes that "don't always hold true," while at the same time acknowledging that there is something useful in understanding broader patterns of behavior and approaches to learning.

A great deal of writing studies research has focused on this dilemma, so there are many resources that might help Charlie. Research looking at quiet students and silence, such as Mary Reda's *Between Speaking and Silence*, Jane Townsend and Danling Fu's "Quiet Students across Cultures and Contexts," Bryan McKinley

Jones Brayboy's "Hiding in the Ivy," and Cheryl Glenn's *Unspoken: A Rhetoric of Silence*, might help Charlie to understand why students are quiet and to learn from experienced teachers who have developed effective classroom strategies. Other resources that reimagine what it means to participate in class, such as Margaret Price's *Mad at School*, might help Charlie envision other ways of engaging students. Each of these texts suggests ways of approaching quiet students and highlights the rich variation within that classification. In addition, Charlie would benefit from ongoing conversations with fellow writing teachers, who all have different vantage points from which they perceive and respond to quiet students.

But how is Charlie to return to his classroom with these rich new resources in mind? He cannot simply assume that the students he has read about in the literature or heard about from his colleagues will explain the students he meets in his classroom. As Glenn and others have shown, silence is a richly rhetorical act. Therefore, being quiet in class must be contextualized and understood through both individual performances *and* broader representations. Even when "classroom silence" is framed as a rich, complex, and situated rhetorical performance, Charlie still needs resources that will help him translate between his own knowledge about quiet students and the unique moment-by-moment negotiations that lead to performances of silence. In other words, how might what Charlie already knows or what he comes to learn be brought to bear on his interactions with individual students? And, considered from another direction, how might these interactions help (re)shape his knowledge about types of students in his classroom?

These are questions about essentialism and determinism as well as about how individual identities and experiences intersect with broader cultural categories. As Helen Fox notes, cultural groups are often described as "'traditional' or unchanging, rather than as systems that blend and shift in response to pressures from the environment and their own members' ingenuity" (259). Such framing of cultural groups in relatively static terms highlights one of the challenges faced by contemporary writing studies scholars: that of using discourses about difference to attend simultaneously to broad group characteristics and to instability within categories. To address this issue, many writing researchers have described their own complex relationships to language, identity, and knowledge (e.g., hooks; Okawa; Villanueva; Young). However, writing teachers—particularly those new to teaching, like Charlie—frequently express anxiety about bringing this nuance and richness into classroom practice. Such nuance is especially needed in contexts where issues of discrimination may make it difficult to recognize problematic patterns, omissions, and/or silences. It is also needed in this current era of data-driven policy, as Patrick Sullivan and David Nielsen point out in their critique of using predictive measures such as standardized test scores to determine access to higher education.

To more fully respond to questions about how awareness of broad identity categories matters when we stand in front of a classroom, talk one-on-one with students, or respond to student writing, what is needed is a flexible means for examining and re-examining the interplay between identity categories and the communicative performances and contexts in which those categories become meaningful. This interplay constitutes what feminist literary theorist Rosaura Sánchez calls a kind of self-reflexivity about identity. She explains, "In the absence of reflexivity, identification is not problematic and identity is a nonissue, as is often the case for Latinos/as who have been isolated in white communities of the Midwest" (41). In other words, their identification as "Latinos/as" is not something frequently called to their attention or held at the forefront of their awareness. However, when these midwesterners relocate "to the southwest or to a large metropolis and they are stopped by the police or are discriminated at work or at a coffee shop as people of color, . . . they become suddenly acutely aware of the identification process and of their designation as members of a particular group" (41). In this new context, being Latino/a has different meanings, and different consequences, for those who identify or are identified by others in that way. Thus, the kinds of things that people notice and the meanings associated with those noticings are highly contingent.

In turn, when Charlie notices his students' quietness as well as their geographic origins, that noticing happens within a particular frame and is influenced and contextualized by many factors. These factors include the institutional setting as well as Charlie's identity and past educational experiences. Such identifications are made not only by those who ascribe identities onto people but also by individuals themselves as they realize how they are identified by others. The values associated with particular identities also influence people's willingness to claim or affiliate with them. This need for flexibility in moving between broad classification and situated performance, then, might lead us to examine how Charlie became aware that "quiet students" or "being from out of state" are things for him to notice and pay attention to, as well as what institutional, professional, and personal discourses circulate around "quiet students" and "out of state students." We might also ask how Charlie can learn from his students how particular categories are meaningful to them.[4]

Such questions have long been central to examinations of difference and diversity in writing pedagogy. Some researchers have addressed these questions by closely studying individual writers or groups of writers to help teachers understand the work these writers are doing and how they are positioned in various ways (e.g., Cushman; Dunn; Lieber; Morris; Purcell-Gates; Sohn); other scholars have built intersectional analyses of how particular group memberships are complexly articulated within writers' lives and discourses (e.g., Alexander; Fernheimer; LeCourt, *Identity*, "Performing"; Royster, *Traces*). In yet another vein of research, scholars examine the means by which individuals communicate across linguistic and cultural differences inside and outside of the classroom (e.g., Flower; Flower, Long, and Higgins; Glazier; Lyons). Taken together, this research on writers, populations, groups, and discourses offers sensitive and nuanced portraits of difference. Despite the many contributions of this body of scholarship, however, teachers like Charlie continue to find it difficult to use it to develop classroom environments sensitive to the ever-changing terrain of difference.

The difficulty teachers experience in moving from research to classroom stems in part from how difference has been framed in writing scholarship. The research described in this introduction urges teachers to develop deep knowledge bases about the students they encounter or are likely to encounter in two primary ways: by becoming more aware of differences that have received little attention and by developing new insights on familiar differences. But at the same time that this research focuses our attention in particular ways, new points of analysis and inquiry are always emerging as significant. While many of us do not shy away from talking about quiet students, other categories, such as race and ethnicity or disability, are not always so easy for us to discuss openly (Brueggemann, White, Dunn, Heifferon, and Cheu; Lewiecki-Wilson and Brueggemann; Lewis, Ketter, and Fabos; Pollock, *Colormute*). What's more, many writing teachers work and live in communities and regions very different from those they are most familiar with. How, then, are teachers to orient to the differences that their unique interactions with students might reveal? Discourses of difference that fix individual writers or groups of writers in time and space can frustrate, rather than enable, the development of pedagogical resources that attend simultaneously to the broad categories that shape our perception of the world *and* to the highly individual encounters we experience on a daily basis.

In this book, my aim is to show how a specific focus on interactionally emergent and rhetorically negotiated elements of a communicative situation can enrich the study of difference in composition research. As part of this project, in this introduction I identify two strategies writing researchers use to forward new understandings of difference that take identity categories as a central unit of analysis and interpretation. These two strategies contribute to the problem of fixing difference in order to study it. The phrase "fixing difference" here refers both to the process of treating difference as a stable thing or property that can be identified and fixed in place as well as to attempts to fix—that is, improve—the way difference is understood.

To move away from this difference fixation, which pervades institutional diversity discourse, as Chapter 1 shows, I build on writing scholarship that takes as a central focus the articulation of change and argue that teachers and researchers should orient to difference as rhetorically negotiated through "marking difference."

When marking difference, speakers and audiences alike display and respond to markers of difference, those rhetorical cues that signal the presence of difference between two or more participants. My own identity as a deaf woman has contributed to the development of this theory, as I regularly find myself making minute adjustments in response to unfolding awareness of how others perceive my deafness and assume its relevance for our interactions.

I draw on my own experiences in Chapter 2, as well as analyses of classroom encounters in a first-year writing classroom in Chapters 3 and 4, to illustrate this perspective on difference, showing that even in the smallest moments of communication—as students debate the placement of a comma, tell stories about their high school writing experiences, try to explain their interpretation of a sentence, or write comments on peers' essays—markers of difference make visible the dynamism, the relationality, and the emergence of difference. Attention to marking difference, when performed in conjunction with attention to various identification processes, can help us mediate between broad conceptual tools for talking about difference and the unique qualities of individual moments of interaction.

Marking difference can reveal a way to simultaneously attend to the myriad resources available for working through our own and our students' classroom identities (i.e., the scholarly literature, our personal experiences, and our colleagues' and students' perspectives) and to the specific and situated classroom encounters in which we and our students bring differences alive. Markers of difference can provide a new set of tools for tracing and analyzing patterns in how we might understand one another.

WRITING RESEARCH AND DIFFERENCE

To understand more specifically some limitations in the way difference is addressed in writing research, I draw on representative examples from the scholarly literature that reveal two ways that teachers are invited to orient to difference in their classrooms: by taxonomizing difference and by performing categorical redefinition. Taxonomizing difference highlights intersections among various identity categories. These intersections enrich the study of identity by acknowledging and recognizing the variety of ways that people can be identified and named. While taxonomizing tends to focus on individuals or small groups of very specific types of people, categorical redefinition focuses on broader groups (although sometimes by studying only a few representatives) to better understand the range and richness of that group.

The practice of taxonomizing difference is illustrated in Esha Niyogi De and Donna Uthus Gregory's essay, "Decolonizing the Classroom," which urges us to develop more complex understandings of students' relationships to academic discourse by considering additional categorical identifications and their intersections. For instance, at one point the authors note that "a rural white student may be further removed from university discourse than a Chinese American student whose parents are college educated professionals" (122). Thus, by naming students' race or ethnicity alongside their place of origin and their parents' educational backgrounds, De and Gregory resist a simplistic link between students' racial/ethnic background and their presumed competence in academic discourse. In pushing for richer understandings, they invoke not only gender, race, ethnicity, and socioeconomic class affiliation, but also religion, course of study, place of residence, patterns of migration, and experiences with formal education. The expansion of available categories refuses to treat racial and ethnic categories as monolithic or governed by stereotypes by recognizing the variation within these categories. In this way, taxonomizing difference complicates the assumptions that shape our first impressions of students. But these categories are presented as relatively static referents, as if there is some enduring stability tied to "white female art major" or "rural Vietnamese student" or "Latino student who grew up in an urban ghetto" (122–23) that we can consequently identify, unpack, and understand. This view is reinforced as De and Gregory refer to these factors as "determinants," effectively calling on inert categorical resources as a way of "determining" the positions available to students (123).

While writing research that looks at various (and increasingly specific) categories of difference takes seriously the need to consider complicated interrelationships among the many factors that influence individuals' orientations to their world and to one another, the focus, as we see in De and Gregory's essay, tends to be placed on categorical identifications that get imposed upon a situation rather than on differences that emerge over the course of interpersonal interaction. By suggesting that differences emerge during interactions, what I mean is that any understanding of a student's academic preparation will be affected by who that student is interacting with as well as the backdrop against which those interactions are occurring. The influence such backdrops can have on students' learning is powerfully illustrated in psychologist Claude Steele's study of what he calls "identity contingencies—the things you have to deal with in a situation because you have a given social identity" (3). Steele finds that being aware of negative stereotypes held by others in particular situations adversely impacts an individual's performance. Therefore, even in the examples cited by De and Gregory of "white female art major" or "rural Vietnamese student" or "Latino student who grew up in an urban ghetto" (122–23), how those identities will matter to or impact a situation is contingent on different interlocutors with a range of orientations to, knowledge about, and personal experiences with those identity categories. Environmental and institutional contexts matter, too. At majority-White colleges and universities, for example, different stereotypes may be more prominent or more threatening than at institutions with larger populations of students of color.

Recognizing the contingency of identity and remaining vigilant toward our own orientations to difference is important for us as teachers because our vantage points lead us to see our students in particular ways—some of which can be harmful and damaging (see Dryer; Schroeder). In his ethnographic study of American Indian students at Ivy League universities, Brayboy points out that these students are noticed by the (mostly White) others on their campuses both because of their physical appearance and because of the ways they comport themselves. But, he notes, interpretations of these students are "based marginally on the ways they present themselves and more substantially on the background, experiences, and visions of the seer, as well as the context in which they are being seen" (130). In pointing out the significance of others' perceptions, Brayboy also reminds us of the power asymmetries involved in managing perception and self-identifications. Our ability to claim particular self-constructions and to have those self-constructions recognized by others is always mediated by the power dynamics influencing an interaction. In classrooms, power asymmetries between teachers and students as well as among students can make such negotiations complex and at times fraught. Therefore, it is not enough for us to simply seek out additional identifiers and cues that we can use to position or better understand our students.

As feminist intersectional analysts have shown, people's relationships to multiple identity categories are not discrete, but instead intermingle, so that, for instance, as legal scholar Kimberlé Williams Crenshaw writes, black women's lives cannot be "captured wholly by looking separately at the race or gender dimensions of those experiences" (358). This is precisely the point De and Gregory are encouraging: teachers need to consider their students not in terms of single identifiers but as the embodiment of a complex set of identifications that must be considered together, rather than independently from one another. The strength of this approach is that it broadens the range of interpretive possibilities. Rather than allowing any given classification to determine a teacher's assessment of a student, the rich confluence of multiple factors holds open more potential directions for an interaction and enables greater consideration of the complexity of identity (see McCall). When identifying students using static determinants, however, taxonomizing difference also focuses from the outset on particular identity categories, which can make it difficult to identify other relevant, but not-already-taxonomized, factors influencing classroom interactions.

A second strategy proffered by writing scholars for encouraging attention to difference, categorical redefinition, also draws heavily on category language for orienting to difference. But unlike taxonomizing difference, which emphasizes multiple categories and their intersections, categorical redefinition focuses on producing more refined and careful interpretations within a specific category. An example of categorical redefinition that reveals how strongly we can be bound by categories even when making explicit efforts to untangle category associations is Christina Ortmeier-Hooper's "English May Be My Second Language, but I'm Not 'ESL.'" Embarking on a study of second language writers in college classrooms, Ortmeier-Hooper notes that learning more information about students can help us better understand our students' classroom behaviors. Here she suggests the incompleteness of categorical understandings: simply labeling a student as "ESL" or "Generation 1.5" or "second language writer" or "bilingual" can lead us to make problematic assumptions about that student's language competencies or classroom needs. However, she asserts, those assumptions might be revised with deeper knowledge and better understanding of the variation within those labels. The bulk of Ortmeier-Hooper's essay focuses on challenging the boundaries of an institutionally ascribed "English as a Second Language" (ESL) label through careful profiles of three writing students, Sergej, Misha, and Jane. Through these profiles, she makes the claim that teachers and researchers need to consider a wider variety of factors relevant to ESL students' performances in the writing classroom, specifically urging us to better understand students' histories and to cultivate an "appreciation" for complexity in students' lives (414–15). With this personal knowledge of students as "whole individuals" rather than as "products of their native culture and language," we can challenge the limitations of traditional understandings of ESL.

But the language Ortmeier-Hooper employs to develop her argument makes it impossible to escape the ESL category for Sergej, Misha, and Jane, as well as for countless other students who may want to resist the predictive (in)validity of a particular label. Consider Sergej's case. He, like Jane and Misha, does not identify himself as "ESL" and resists being identified by others in that way. And indeed, Ortmeier-Hooper convincingly establishes that his cultural expectations of schooling, as well as his experiences with war and violence, more so than his status as an ESL student, shape his attitudes toward his teacher and his writing. But instead of working to identify how well—or not well—he fits the institutional ESL label, we might instead consider the ways that Sergej himself made claims about what was important or salient to his identity: How did he display himself to the others in the classroom? How did he position himself—directly and indirectly—among fellow classmates and teachers? What cues did he identify as important or significant in doing this work? The question of what kinds of frames are most useful for understanding Sergej's experiences is worth interrogating further.

Research such as Ortmeier-Hooper's is motivated by a desire to understand and work with a particular group or category of students, not out of a desire to impose labels on students. Yet the line between imposing labels on students and understanding them better is not always clear. Ortmeier-Hooper herself sheds light on the problematic nature of ESL as a category as she writes, "Often, we fail to recognize that 'ESL' refers to a great deal more than language proficiency or placement" (394). She consequently urges broader acknowledgment of ESL's vast array of identifiers and meanings.[5] The result of this rhetorical move, however, is that students like Sergej, who claim to fall outside the label's bounds, are ultimately brought back within its folds simply because we have redefined ESL to include considerations of how different cultural orientations influence students' classroom performances. Despite Ortmeier-Hooper's own recognition of the ESL category's limitations, her response to the problem of the category that no longer fits is to redefine the category to give it new connotations and different institutional resonance.[6]

Thus, even as taxonomizing difference and redefining categories have enhanced the way we teach with and across differences, these approaches to studying and writing about difference still freeze particular subjects, details, and interpretations within the research literature. Yet this scholarship, which creates a more precise language for difference and offers nuanced portrayals of various identity categories, is not motivated by a desire to freeze differences in time and space, but instead by a desire to open up new interpretive ground and broaden the range of potential meanings within categorical frames. Indeed, writing researchers have taken numerous approaches to documenting ongoing transformations of meaning, in many cases influenced by ethnographic research methods and methodologies (Brown and Dobrin; Lillis) and an explosion of writing research looking at writing in context (see Juzwik, Curcic, Wolbers, Moxley, Dimling, and Shankland for an overview). Key to these efforts is attention to flexibility and change. In *Rhetorical Listening*, for example, Krista Ratcliffe challenges the logic of Whiteness, which she defines as "a trope that fosters stasis by resisting and denying differences" (114), and urges her readers to employ a variety of means of rhetorical listening to resist such fixity. Listening is always situational, she notes, always in the moment. This emphasis on situatedness is also evident in performance-based analyses that focus on how individuals artfully use particular resources at particular times for particular audiences to create specific identities (Gonçalves). Numerous scholars have enacted such performances by narrating their experiences in order to counter or disrupt dominant interpretations (Craig and Perryman-Clark; Royster, "When"; M. Powell). Other writing scholars use revision as a trope for understanding the creation and re-creation of identity through writing (Herrington and Curtis; Jung; Lee; Young). In literacy studies, researchers such as Suzanne Rumsey and Gail Hawisher and Cynthia Selfe have examined how multimodal forms of literacy (e.g., quilting and online social networks) reveal identity building and literacy transmission as unpredictable and dynamic processes. Finally, some scholars have begun to incorporate time as a dimension for interpreting classroom activity in order to describe identity construction as an ongoing process occurring across different timescales (cf. Lemke) in classrooms and through writing (Burgess and Ivanič; Wortham, *Learning*).

Despite the acknowledgments made within this research regarding continual change, resistance, and transformation through language, there remain questions about how we might make best use of this research to improve our pedagogical practices. Taxonomizing difference and categorical redefinition are in many ways part of human behavior and sense-making. As sociologist and gender theorist Cecilia Ridgeway explains in *Framed by Gender*, "social relations are situations in which people form a sense of who they are in the situation and, therefore, how they should behave, by considering themselves in relation to whom they assume others are in that situation" (6–7). But the details we notice and consequently use to define ourselves and others, as well as the associations and meanings we attribute to these noticings, are affected by a wide variety of factors, including personal and professional experiences and academic scholarship.

Our own positioning as teachers and its influence on what we "know" when we read student writing or work with students in the classroom is pointedly illustrated in an example from the scholarly literature. Janis Haswell and Richard Haswell describe the results of a study in which they asked sixty-four readers to respond to two student texts, provide suggestions for revision, and discuss their impressions of the students' gender. They found that the respondents drew on broad gender stereotypes to interpret these texts and offer revision suggestions. Haswell and Haswell's results dovetail with Ridgeway's work on the persistence of gender inequality. Ridgeway shows how individuals negotiate new situations by framing them with cultural beliefs—i.e., stereotypes—about gender that consequently reinforce these beliefs and maintain gender inequality.

Identifying categories and drawing on simplistic cultural beliefs or stereotypes to interpret those categories is not the only way students' writing and experiences are fixed in time and space, however. A second problematic strategy is that of overidentification. This is a problem that Donna LeCourt describes in her work with working-class students, as she acknowledges how hard it is to avoid assuming or presuming to "know" her students. She writes, "I have to constantly guard against assuming that my own experience as a student from the working class will also explain my students'." She continues, "Listening for difference, frankly, is difficult. I have to remind myself that being open and student-centered is not enough" ("Performing" 49). These are key challenges for all of us as we pay close attention to issues of identity and difference both in and out of the writing classroom.

The current focus on difference in writing studies has prepared teachers to attend to particular details, and it has reinforced the need to continually become aware of new ones—that is, to hold open interpretations rather than presume understanding—but it has not yet fully articulated *how* such new interpretations might be built. This book, then, suggests a new rhetoric of difference through which we can cultivate awareness of new details, interpret and reinterpret those details, and contextualize them within specific moments of writing, teaching, and learning. This perspective complements broader identification processes and offers a means for carefully enriching those identifications through attention to the lived experiences that bring differences alive in the classroom.

Such mediation acknowledges the vital role categories play in the negotiation of everyday life. Individuals perceive categories as they make decisions about how to negotiate interactions. This work is not always done consciously, although various contextual factors and identity contingencies (Steele) affect the degree to which people hold particular identities at the forefront of their awareness during unfolding interactions. The research presented in this book aims to encourage heightened awareness of systematic patterns of ignoring, suppressing, and denying difference as well as of recognizing, highlighting, and orienting to difference. Such engagement is sorely needed among both teachers and students in writing classrooms.

STUDYING THE ENGAGEMENT OF DIFFERENCE

In designing a study aimed at better understanding how teachers, especially those new to the profession, might engage the differences they encounter between themselves and their students, I began with the concept of difference itself, asking:

- How is difference identified within classrooms?
- What conditions or factors motivate engagement with difference?

These questions concern not only teachers' interactions with students but also students' interactions with one another. If, as Paula Moya asserts, "a truly multi-perspectival, multicultural education will work to *mobilize* identities in the classroom" (96), then it is essential for both students and teachers to engage one another in a variety of ways. Two theories prevalent in writing studies research articulate the importance of engagement with others to writing: dialogism (Dyson; Halasek; Nystrand, "Dialogic," *Opening*) and contact zones (Pratt; Wolff). Both theories emphasize the centrality of writer–audience relationships. Dialogism is concerned with how written and spoken discourses respond to past utterances and anticipate responses from others, while contact zones take seriously issues of audience quality and exposure to diverse perspectives. These two bodies of scholarship deeply informed the following questions, which served as guides for the empirical study I designed. Choosing to focus on institutional diversity discourses alongside students' interactions with one another in the writing classroom, I asked:

- How do students engage difference in higher education?
- What role—if any—does writing play in students' engagement with difference?

To maximize the likelihood of observing substantive engagement with difference, I situated my study in a classroom I thought would be most likely to sponsor such engagement. The classroom I chose was a first-year composition course that involved students in processes of argumentation and orienting to multiple perspectives. Taught by a well-respected and experienced teacher, the class was also part of a university-wide diversity initiative that established living–learning communities. The increased familiarity among students due to three shared courses and proximate living arrangements, paired with the academic topics under discussion, would, I believed, make this classroom a fertile ground for observing sustained interaction and engagement among students.

I hypothesized that the study would reveal interactions that spoke to broader categories, such as conversations about gender, race, and ethnicity, or encounters that directly or indirectly invoked identity-related issues, particularly because of the content of the courses in which students were enrolled. However, attention to difference between students was far more subtle than explicit reference to categorical identity signifiers. Students in the writing classroom I studied rarely publicly named their own or others' race, ethnicity, gender, disability, sexuality, or socioeconomic class affiliations. While people regularly use category identifiers to name their own and others' identities (see, e.g., DeFina; West and Fenstermaker; Pollock, *Colormute*), the use of such identifiers in students' classroom talk may have been tempered by the institutional setting of this study: a majority-White midwestern university. In her study of racial signifiers at an urban high school, educational anthropologist Mica Pollock notes the persistence of silence on racial questions and issues among the mostly White teachers and administrators at the school. For those teachers and administrators, talking about race was fraught with risk. These risks included the fear of being called racist, the fear of essentializing racial identity, and the fear of ignoring all aspects of race (or of being overly focused on just one). As Pollock writes, "With bystanders always ready to contest the accuracy or appropriateness of any proffered description of how race mattered, the overwhelming social complexity of race talk might stifle your willingness to analyze such stories in racial terms at all" (*Colormute* 213).

Whether or not identity categories are an explicit topic of discussion, such category identifications are nevertheless part of the classroom environment. As students perceive one another in the classroom through the sound of their voices, their physical appearance, material possessions, and classroom comportment, they also apprehend gender, racial, ethnic, and other group affiliations and use those identifications to help organize their interactions. That students did not explicitly name such categories during the classroom conversations I recorded may not be all that surprising. After all, despite the fact that college and university campuses are often promoted as free and open spaces for deliberation and engaging ideas, they have not traditionally been seen as safe places for race talk, especially at majority-White institutions like the one studied here. We need look no further than Kristen Myers's *Racetalk: Racism Hiding in Plain Sight* or Eduardo Bonilla-Silva's *Racism without Racists* to find examples of racist ideologies and discourses that are part of the fabric of contemporary college life.

In the context of these pervasive social attitudes, having public dialogues about race may seem an impossibility. That such dialogues are necessary, however, is illustrated by writing teachers and scholars who acknowledge the dynamics of campus discourse and the challenges students face in trying to productively intervene in racist discourse (Hoang; P. Powell). The public nature of classroom interaction, even within the relatively private realm of small-group peer review workshops (and perhaps especially in situations that students know are being recorded), may be an arena in which students are unwilling to take too many social risks with their discourse. However, although the students in this classroom were verbally silent on many issues of race and other contested identities, their interactions with one another were *not* silent regarding how they positioned themselves and others even if they did not—at least in the sessions I recorded—openly use category identifiers to accomplish such positions.

What students' interactions during small-group peer review did reveal was a complex dynamic in which relationships and positions, the very material of identity formation, emerged during interaction. Indeed, students worked hard during peer review to establish desirable positions alongside their classmates and to construct identities that their peers would find persuasive. These acts of identity construction took place against a backdrop of living and learning at a majority-White institution midway through a major diversity initiative. This institutional context powerfully oriented students and teachers toward particular ways of thinking and talking about race and other differences. While institutional discourses are created by social actors who operate within the institution, these discourses also influence and shape individuals' talk. Consequently, attention to students' and teachers' classroom discourse must be considered within the context of the discourses that circulate at this institution.

STUDY DESIGN AND IMPLEMENTATION

When I began this study, I wanted to learn from participants what differences were relevant to them and how those differences became apparent and meaningful. Toward that end, I took cues from ethnomethodologists' orientation to participants as "informants" who can help analysts better understand how people participate in everyday communicative activities (Garfinkel). Communication does not just happen but is part of a process that is co-constructed by all participants. Further, because interactions are strongly influenced by the contexts in which they happen—e.g., in writing classrooms, at large majority-White public universities, in the Midwest—paying careful attention to how such contexts shape participants' orientation to an activity is important.

This study took place during the 2003 fall semester at a large midwestern university that I am calling Midwestern University (MU). Members of MU's entering class that fall had an average ranking in the 89th percentile of their high school classes and an average SAT score of 1260, both of which reveal MU to be a selective public institution. In the 2003–04 academic year, slightly more than half of MU's total student population was female (53 percent), and the racial/ethnic breakdown was 86.6 percent White/Other,[7] 2.4 percent African American; 4.7 percent Asian American (including 1.2 percent Southeast Asian American); 0.5 percent American Indian; 2.5 percent Latino/a; and 3.3 percent international. At the time of this study, the university was actively working to change the composition of its student body through a large-scale diversity agenda.

As part of this agenda, the institution sponsored several diversity initiatives aimed at improving the representation of four underrepresented student groups: American Indian, African American, Southeast Asian American, and Latino/a. The largest diversity initiative within the College of Arts and Sciences, a First-Year Experience (FYE) program, established living and learning communities in which students enrolled in a shared set of courses and lived near one another in proximate dormitories. The year this study was conducted was the third year the FYE program was in operation; it included 470 students participating in twenty-four different course clusters ranging broadly in topic and content.[8]

FYE students, like MU students generally, were an accomplished group. The 2003 FYE report noted that the composite ACT score of FYE participants was 27.2 and that nearly half—43.6 percent—of the fall 2003 FYE cohort graduated in the top tenth of their class. These numbers were nearly identical to the composite ACT of 27.3 for the incoming MU class, of whom 42.9 percent graduated in the top tenth of their class. Where the FYE program's demographics diverged from MU's general first-year population was in gender, race, and ethnicity. While MU's incoming class had an overall gender distribution that was 54 percent male and 46 percent female, the FYE cohort was more than two-thirds female (68 percent). The FYE cohort was also composed of 16 percent ethnic minority students, whereas MU's first-year cohort was 11 percent ethnic minority (although which groups "ethnic minority" designates is not defined in the FYE end-of-semester report from which these data are taken).

MU's First-Year Composition (FYC) program is housed within the English department, administered by a faculty director and two graduate student assistant directors. At the time of this study, the core of the program's approach to teaching composition was a model syllabus based on philosopher Stephen Toulmin's theory of argument.[9] All first-time teaching assistants were required to use the model syllabus, and even when given independence in syllabus design, many continued to draw from its approach as they developed their own syllabi. The three major essay assignments in the model syllabus asked students to move from analyzing arguments to producing lengthier research-based arguments of their own. Each paper assignment involved two rounds of peer review, and approximately one-quarter of the class sessions in the model syllabus course calendar were devoted to peer review activities.

In fall 2003, ten sections of FYC were linked to FYE course clusters. I approached several instructors teaching these courses about participating in my study, and Yvonne, a White graduate student with five semesters of experience teaching First-Year Composition, responded eagerly. Yvonne's FYC course was linked to a small psychology seminar led by a faculty member and a large sociology lecture with graduate assistant–led discussion sections.

The class was populated by nineteen students, fourteen women and five men. Thirteen of the students were White, one was Asian American, and five were members of one of the four ethnic groups that were the focus of Midwestern's diversity agenda—one African

American, two Hispanic, and two Southeast Asian American students. Fifteen students indicated their age as eighteen at the start of the semester, three were nineteen, and one left that question blank.[10] Sixteen students came from Midwestern's home state, and three came from other states in the Midwest. Of the seventeen students who indicated their high school ranking, all finished in the top half of their high school graduating classes. Fifteen of those seventeen placed in the top 20 percent of their graduating classes. Nine students came from a high school with between 300 and 500 students in their graduating class. Three graduated with classes of less than 100, six had graduating classes consisting of between 100 and 300 students, and one had a graduating class of more than 500 students.

Data Generation

Over the course of this study, I generated a wide range of data.

- I attended and audiotaped every class session and took field notes.
- I video- and audiotaped at least one peer review workshop group during each of ten peer review sessions, for a total of thirteen recorded peer review workshops.
- I collected students' demographic information through a written survey.
- I collected or photocopied all curricular materials distributed in class.
- I collected and photocopied all of the students' paper portfolios at the conclusion of each of three units. These portfolios included Yvonne's feedback and at least two sets of drafts with peer review comments.
- I conducted two sixty- to ninety-minute interviews with four focal students, for a total of eight audio-recorded interviews.[11]
- I conducted and audio-recorded two ninety-minute interviews with Yvonne.
- I collected institutional documents related to MU's diversity agenda, including websites and data reports.

Data Analysis

All the audiotapes of classroom talk, peer review, and interviews were roughly transcribed immediately after each class meeting or interview by a stenographer. These rough transcripts showed the words that were spoken but did not provide full interactional data, including overlapping speech, starts and stops, pauses, or volume. I reviewed these transcripts in between class meetings while writing up field notes and in preparation for interviews. Through this review, I identified moments to play on audiotape for simulated recall during the first round of interviews with focal students in order to garner additional insight on puzzling or difficult interactional moments. The second set of focal student interviews asked students to talk about specific pieces of written feedback as well as to reflect on their participation in the FYE program.

As I worked with the rough transcripts of classroom discourse, I quickly realized I needed much more detail in the transcripts: I needed to know where students were interrupting and overlapping, when they decided to speak, when they remained silent, and how they organized their talk with one another. Because I am deaf, I could not add this detail to the transcripts myself, so I worked with a graduate assistant trained in transcription methodologies to add this detail to the thirteen recorded peer review sessions. She also reviewed the rough transcripts of interviews and class meetings to ensure accuracy and fill in any words or utterances not already transcribed, but she did not add full interactional details to those transcripts. I have some residual hearing that, when amplified with hearing aids, enables me to follow audiotapes and videotapes along with a written transcript in front of me, so once I had a detailed transcript, I verified each line of transcript through my own careful listening. In cases where I had trouble following or disagreed with a particular stretch of transcript, I held meetings with the transcriptionist to conduct reliability checks. In this way, we worked together to arrive at agreement on the transcript's representation of the audio data.

To trace patterns of talk and interaction within the transcripts, I employed transcript conventions developed by conversation analyst

Gail Jefferson (as described in Sacks, Schegloff, and Jefferson) for representing overlapping speech, interruptions, pauses, and other verbal cues. I did not, however, ask my transcriptionist to record some prosodic elements of talk, such as changes in pitch, largely because these were not cues I could verify through my own review of the audio data. Other cues, such as speed of talk, I represent through attention to elongated sounds and the division of transcript lines into "breath units" (Scollon and Scollon). In this structure, each line represents what was said within a single breath, with a slight modification: I also broke lines according to pauses, measuring all pauses that lasted longer than half a second. So a line could be broken because a speaker took a breath or because there was a pause (more than half a second) that punctuated the talk. This organization for transcripts was the most effective for drawing attention to the ways that students patterned their talk (see Chapter 3 for transcript conventions).

Tenets of grounded theory (Strauss and Corbin) guided my initial orientation to the range of data I collected. I began by looking for where and how students called attention to difference in their peer review interactions, interview data, and classroom participation. The first layer of coding revealed two genres of interaction in which students displayed difference most prominently: telling stories and disagreeing. In subsequent rounds of coding, I extracted narratives and episodes of disagreement from the data for closer analysis (see Chapter 3 for more detail on these genres and their identification and analysis).

In performing these more fine-grained analyses of students' peer review talk, I drew on a variety of tools for performing dialogic discourse analysis of classroom talk (Nystrand, "Dialogic," *Opening*; Rex and Juzwik). Central to developing my analyses were methods of studying indexicality, contextualization, and positioning developed in sociolinguistics and linguistic anthropology (Bamberg, "Positioning"; Duranti and Goodwin; Georgakopoulou, *Small*, "Styling"; Silverstein and Urban; Wortham, *Narratives, Learning*). Attention to these resources helped me to understand how students used their talk to point to or make relevant various elements of the surrounding talk and interactional context in order to communicate how their utterances should be interpreted. These resources also illuminated what students were cueing as significant in their own and others' self-presentations. Complementing the linguistic tools I used to parse the interactional data, I employed methods of critical discourse analysis (Gee) to unpack institutional talk about diversity that circulated at MU.

Incubating the Study

The preceding description of the various methodological and analytic steps I have taken in my data analysis and writing represents only part of the picture of the development of this book. The fact is, writing this book was a long time in the making. In the ten years that have elapsed since conducting this study and the emergence of this book, I have come to a much richer, more nuanced, and more complex articulation of difference than the one I started with when I designed the study. This has by no means been a linear trajectory: my experience writing this book has been as filled with bumps and setbacks as it has been with movement and development. I have come to recognize in my early writing on this topic a stance shaped as much by the audiences engaging with my research as by my own thinking. The more audiences that have responded and spoken to my thinking, the more my writing has taken up new and richer nuance. Perhaps the most significant step I took in developing this work, however, was to seriously examine my own orientation to thinking about difference.

From the outset of this project, numerous readers asked me to address my deafness and its relationship to the work I was doing. I resisted that move, for a variety of reasons, but one of the most significant was that I didn't think I was conducting a study about myself. But that sense of detachment was the very thing—or one of the main things—that kept me from really understanding that my experience of deafness was not just something that happened to me, but also something that others took up in various and complicated ways (Kerschbaum, "On Rhetorical"). Until I did this work, I did not fully recognize how my own interactional preferences gave me a stake in the findings I was sharing and disseminating. As a deaf woman who is often the only deaf person in the room, I routinely encounter others who have relatively little knowledge about what my deafness might mean for our interactions. Therefore, like countless others, I want my interlocutors to take my accommodation needs and interactional preferences seriously. Above all, I want them to avoid assuming that they know better than I do how I prefer to communicate and be identified. But in my desire for self-autonomy and self-identification, I failed to consider the significance of others' identifications of me. This is reflected in an early stance I took that privileged students' claims about identity while attending less to the work teachers do in identifying students in productive—and yes, at times unproductive—ways. Indeed, as teachers we are sometimes wrong in the identifications we make of our students, but we are not *always* so.

A second shift I made in my thinking came out of an early emphasis I placed on inexperienced teachers as an audience for this research. When I began this project, I was not focused on the ways that experienced teachers have deep knowledge bases that enrich their ability to respond to and engage students. However, as I myself have gained experience teaching writing at three different institutions in different parts of the country, my thinking about markers of difference in the classroom has changed. In embracing the work of experience, I have cultivated ways of listening to the various pedagogical stories and teacher narratives told by teachers across our profession. These stories illuminate the variety and richness of markers of difference, and they suggest ways that markers of difference can be a powerful pedagogical resource for experienced and inexperienced teachers alike.

ORGANIZATION OF THE BOOK

The chapters of this book move from broad context to local situation to examine how difference is experienced in higher education and in writing classrooms. Chapter 1 shows how institutional diversity discourses treat difference as a thing or property. Within higher education, diversity tends to be framed as a goal to work toward or a commodity to accumulate. To illustrate the impact of such commodification, this chapter uses critical discourse analysis to examine Midwestern University's diversity discourses. While diversity discourses are pervasive throughout the academy, such language does not offer university administrators or writing teachers effective tools for imagining pedagogical and university environments sensitive to the situatedness of difference, and it contrasts with the lived experience of difference, to which Chapter 2 turns.

Chapter 2 argues that what is needed is a resource for understanding how differences are negotiated within everyday moments of classroom interaction, as well as how this experience of difference connects with knowledge gleaned through life experience and professional training. Drawing on the ethical writings of Mikhail Bakhtin (*Art, Toward*), this chapter highlights three characteristics of difference—relationality, dynamism, and emergence—that challenge the notion of difference-as-property articulated in institutional diversity rhetoric. Within this framework, individuals are seen as using rhetorical cues, markers of difference, to position themselves alongside others, thus showing difference not as a possession but as an emergent and continually shifting relationship that is constructed through the use and display of markers of difference. This theory is illustrated with personal narratives related to my deafness. This theoretical apparatus enables us as teachers to envision difference rhetorically and thus has promise for renewing our attention to ways that we move and interact with others in the classroom.

To show markers of difference at work, Chapter 3 analyzes two brief moments of student interaction between three women—one White and two Southeast Asian American—during a peer review workshop. The analyses examine minute shifts that occur as students display markers of difference in response to unfolding dialogue. One conversation, about the placement of a comma, foregrounds the interrelationship between personal identity and writing and raises questions about the possibilities of rhetorical agency. The second conversation, an exchange of stories about students' past experiences with writing papers, involves a complicated interplay of sameness and differentiation. Taken together, these analyses show markers of difference as rhetorical resources that are used to construct identifications, project identity categories onto others, and challenge and resist undesirable ascriptions of identity. The chapter concludes by describing three ways markers of difference can improve writing pedagogy: by enabling us to resist simplistic generalizations about students, by helping us identify possibilities for rhetorical agency and open up dialogue, and by providing a means for recognizing and revising ways of interacting in the classroom.

While Chapter 3 emphasizes the possibilities of markers of difference as well as their performative dimensions, Chapter 4 examines two moments of classroom discourse that evoke the limitations of marking difference: what happens when individuals do not openly acknowledge significant differences or when they cannot understand others' markers of difference? The chapter opens by unpacking a conversation between a White woman and a White man in which they perform conflicting readings of a sentence but fail to recognize the other's interpretation. The second analysis looks at how three women in a writing group differently respond to one another's essays, focusing in particular on a Southeast Asian American woman's query to her two White group members about her thesis, a query that is dismissed by the group despite the author's explicit concern. These analyses reveal that markers are sometimes disregarded or misunderstood and gestures toward reasons why some markers are readily identified while others are ignored.

1

The Market for Diversity in Higher Education

WHILE MY PRIMARY GOAL IN STUDYING interactional discourse in a writing classroom was to understand how students engaged issues of difference, those classroom discourses cannot be understood as independent from their institutional contexts. As Sara Ahmed reminds us in her study of diversity discourses in the United Kingdom and Australia, "Institutions provide a frame in which things happen (or don't happen)" (50). Circulating institutional discourses organize people in particular ways, and classroom interactions are shaped by these institutional frames, a point Christopher Schroeder underscores in his institutional case study of "the most ethnically diverse university in the Midwest" (33). To understand how people's institutional experiences orient them toward difference and diversity, I analyze Midwestern University's diversity discourse.

MU's discourses about diversity, including definitions and categories used to account for diversity across campus, can be fruitfully unpacked using methods of critical discourse analysis. Rhetoric scholars have analyzed a variety of institutional discourses, from university presidential addresses (P. Powell) to the United States census (Crable 133–35) to corporate discourse (Mathieu), in order to uncover tacit ideological commitments behind such language use. For instance, Mathieu's analysis of Starbucks shows how the company crafts language practices that create demand for their product and thus promote desirable (for Starbucks) coffee-consumption habits. In its basic form, critical discourse analysis constitutes attention to how language reflects ideologies. When social institutions create and perpetuate particular forms of language, that language is never disinterested. To identify these political and social forces, critical discourse analysts examine naturally occurring language in use. Following James Paul Gee, the analyses in this chapter take as a starting point the idea that all utterances draw on presumed-to-be-shared background knowledge regarding how those utterances should be interpreted, as well as what kind of audiences will receive them. To interpret the meaning of an utterance, then, requires attention to the contexts that shape its meanings. For example, when *diversity* is defined, as it is in numerous places at MU, we might ask who those definitions are for as well as what audiences are imagined by these definitions. These questions probe how meanings are signaled by speakers and their audiences, not just what those meanings are.

Taking a pragmatic approach to such constructions of meaning, sociolinguists Jan Blommaert and Jef Verschueren show how a particular definition is ascribed to the word *migrant* within the context of a long-standing debate over immigrant workers in Belgium. While a technical definition of *migrant worker* might include any person who immigrates to Belgium and gets a job, Blommaert and Verschueren demonstrate that newspaper articles use the word to reference immigrants from a particular geographic region, so that even when the generic word *migrant* is evoked, a specific image comes to readers' minds. Like *migrant, diversity* is a word with many potential meanings that are contextually narrowed through its use in institutional and everyday talk.

To explain how particularities of meaning are communicated within everyday language practice, Gee describes what he calls "cultural models." For Gee, cultural models function as "normalized worlds" in which meanings operate. As long as nothing comes along to disrupt these meanings, people simply assume them to be holding true. So when, for instance, the words *migrant* or *diversity* are used in everyday parlance, people assume that a conventional meaning applies. However, these commonsense meanings, as Blommaert and Verschueren illustrate, can also exclude or marginalize meanings that do not fall within the typical frame. That such constructions of meaning are often tacit and unexamined affords these marginalizations greater influence. Therefore, remaining vigilant toward these often unexamined meanings can help us resist the discriminatory effects of some language uses.

The legal and political debates surrounding diversity on college campuses today make it a particularly important word to critically examine in the manner that Gee and Blommaert and Verschueren describe. Accordingly, this chapter draws on diversity-related documents and discourses collected between 2003 and 2012 at MU to illuminate the implicit and explicit boundaries that circumscribe notions of diversity. I attend to webpages, marketing and promotional brochures, strategic planning materials, annual releases of official university data, published statistics, admissions materials, statements from university leaders and faculty members, and presentations delivered by diversity officials. While this chapter is informed by all of these texts, one item receives particular attention: a sweeping ten-year plan for improving diversity at MU. Renamed here as the Midwestern University Diversity Agenda (MUDA),[1] this plan outlines a set of diversity-related goals largely focused on "four targeted ethnic groups": African American, American Indian, Southeast Asian American, and Latino/a peoples. It also lays the groundwork for numerous initiatives and programs focused on increasing the number of underrepresented students, faculty, and staff on campus.

When I began systematic data collection on this project in 2003, the introduction to the MUDA was *the* most public diversity document at Midwestern University. Disseminated widely across campus, it was reprinted in glossy brochures publicizing the agenda, and it had a prominent home on the provost's website; it represented Midwestern's commitment to diversity, in that almost every website at MU that mentioned diversity either quoted the MUDA introduction or linked back to the provost's website hosting the full introduction. The MUDA officially concluded in the late 2000s, but many of its themes persist in current diversity discourses at Midwestern University.

The analysis that follows certainly critiques diversity discourse at MU, but it is not intended as an untempered criticism of the university nor of specific individuals: the language and discourses within these documents are not the product of any single person or group. They are also not limited to MU, for at the same time that this language guided and shaped talk about diversity on campus, Midwestern's campus discourses were also influenced by national and local conversations about diversity in higher education that have been ongoing and contentious for decades (see, e.g., Karabel; Lemann; Newfield; Padilla and Montiel; Takagi).

This chapter argues that institutional diversity discourses reify and commodify race–ethnic difference and develops that argument through attention to three elements of diversity discourse at Midwestern University: arguments about the importance of diversity, definitions of diversity, and claims about who does diversity and who it is for. Justifying the importance of diversity by drawing on neoliberal discourses reinforces problematic ways of valuing student bodies, and it raises ethical dilemmas that are exacerbated by the traditional means universities employ to account for and define diversity. While *diversity* is often defined broadly depending on context, it is consistently measured by counting the number of students, faculty, and staff belonging to particular race–ethnic categories. Within neoliberal discourses, then, diversity becomes a kind of property that individuals hold by virtue of their race–ethnic backgrounds, and institutions accumulate "diversity capital" by recruiting and retaining members of these race–ethnic categories to campus. Extending this metaphor of group membership as desirable property that can enhance a university's diversity profile, a close analysis of the rhetoric of "targeting" and "being targeted" reveals dramatically different roles vis-à-vis diversity for different groups and individuals at MU. In this language, difference is neither dynamic nor flexible: it is an individual property that institutions covet. When students find themselves defined within institutional category systems, their own self-perceptions and orientations to difference and otherness are affected.

THE MARKET FOR DIVERSITY

In *What Money Can't Buy*, Michael J. Sandel argues that we are moving from "*having* a market economy to *being* a market society"

(10). In a market society, Sandel explains, "market values seep into every aspect of human endeavor. It's a place where social relations are made over in the image of the market" (10–11). Like Sandel, many higher education scholars are troubled by market encroachment into arenas that may not be well governed by market values. For example, Henry Giroux argues that the intrusion of corporate culture and neoliberal discourse into the university reflects a corrosion of the democratic values at the heart of public education. Noting what he calls the "commodification of language," which frames "admitting college students as 'closing a deal,' and university presidents as CEOs" (430), he suggests that such language heralds a decline in the university's commitment to values such as liberal education or learning as a form of civic participation.

The incursion of market values into diversity discourses is clearly illustrated through what has come to be known as "the diversity rationale" following a series of Supreme Court cases on affirmative action in higher education (Regents of the University of California v. Bakke; Gratz v. Bollinger et al.; Grutter v. Bollinger et al.; Fisher v. University of Texas at Austin et al.). These Supreme Court cases have consistently affirmed diversity as the key motivation for considering race in university admissions, and increasingly, that claim is reinforced with market justifications. Supreme Court Justice Sandra Day O'Connor explicitly links diversity and the market when she writes in her majority decision in the Grutter case that the University of Michigan Law School's commitment to diversity is

> bolstered by numerous expert studies and reports showing that such diversity promotes learning outcomes and *better prepares students for an increasingly diverse workforce*, for society, and for the legal profession. *Major American businesses have made clear that the skills needed in today's increasingly global marketplace* can only be developed through exposure to widely diverse people, cultures, ideas, and viewpoints. (emphasis added)

O'Connor frames diversity here as necessary for preparing students for the contemporary workforce, which is imagined as part of an "increasingly global marketplace."

Discourse linking diversity and market values is common at Midwestern. For example, a section of the MUDA introduction titled "Why We Must Work for Greater Diversity on This Campus" offers "three reasons why this plan is important":

1. to provide educational success for students from targeted ethnic groups in our state and nation who still suffer the social, economic, and educational consequences of discrimination;
2. to diversify the students, faculty, and staff to better reflect the overall population distribution, which has educational value for all of us by providing a multitude of perspectives and the opportunity for healthy inter-group relations;
3. *to better prepare our students to be more competitive for future work and career possibilities in a global economy* and to be better citizens in a multi-cultural global community. (emphasis added)

The first reason draws on the language of social justice and inequity to address racism and other forms of discrimination; the second is a rearticulation of part of the diversity rationale—that diversity among students, faculty, and staff is necessary for enabling inter-group contact and engagement. The third reason invokes a neoliberal framework, emphasizing the university's role as a career preparation center as well as students' pragmatic desire to successfully find employment after college.

On the surface, invoking a link between market values and diversity may seem to be an effective way to convey the importance of diversity to *all* members of the campus, including White students, who may be skeptical about the value of affirmative action programs. Encouraging White students to support diversity is not only important because of the Supreme Court's insistence that universities show diversity as a collective rather than an individual benefit (see Liu), but also because, as educational researcher Uma Jayakumar writes, "court decisions advancing civil rights for people of color in the United States have most often occurred when such decisions also served the best interest of the dominant group" (624). And yet, though it is certainly important to garner White students' support for institutional diversity, the language of the market troubles, rather than solidifies, a commitment to the issues of inequality and social justice that motivate affirmative action programs.

To understand the incongruity between justifications for diversity based on social justice or educational quality and justifications for diversity that draw on market values, let's take a look at what is a now-dominant political and economic philosophy: neoliberalism. Neoliberalism orients to individuals on the basis of their value for economic markets. Central to neoliberalism are beliefs in individual ownership of property and limited government regulation, assuming, as geographer David Harvey puts it, that "the social good will be maximized by maximizing the reach and frequency of market transactions" (3).

While some scholars have welcomed neoliberal orientations to higher education, others ask the same questions Sandel poses: Is our transformation into a "market society" a positive one? Are there things that money should not buy, transactions that should not be governed by the market? More important for this discussion, I ask what happens when diversity discourses draw on market rhetorics and justifications? There are many examples of such market discourses at MU. Casual references to the market or to students' involvement in a "global community" pervade MU's diversity rhetoric. On a website titled "Diversity in Admissions," a definition of diversity mentions four educational benefits, including that diversity helps "prepare citizens and leaders for the global community." A statement showcased on the university's diversity website proclaims,

> We live in a diverse society that is increasingly interconnected with the political, cultural, and economic interests of people in other parts of the world. Educating graduates who are prepared to live in this global environment requires that we foster and celebrate the diversity among human beings and cultures. ("Provost's")

A 2009 letter to the campus community highlights the importance of higher education to this "global" society: "We know that higher education has never been more important than it is today, when global economic shifts have changed the nature of work and the skills required of our workforce" ("To the [Midwestern] Community"). In a list of five "strategic diversity interests" posted on the Office for Diversity website, the fourth item is "preparing all our students, staff, and faculty to thrive personally and professionally in a world that is diverse, global, and interconnected" ("Office for Diversity"). Finally, the MUDA introduction quotes a former administrator who asserts that diversity "makes us more competitive among our peer institutions," adding, "if we are to be successful in the future, we must tap the rich potential of all our citizens by incorporating them into our faculty, staff, and student body." Again: diversity contributes to the university's success and stature, and the university must "tap" this resource to convert it to institutional gain.

Unfortunately, when diversity is articulated through the language of the global market, as in these examples, the effect is to commodify individuals' racial and ethnic backgrounds. In such discourses, linguistic anthropologist Bonnie Urciuoli explains, *diversity* is "defined as bits of cultural difference possessed by an individual" and "is valued not in its own right but as something potentially productive" ("Neoliberal" 175). Thus, while MU "targets" specific student and faculty bodies to achieve diversity goals, the articulation of these goals within the discourse of neoliberalism converts those individual backgrounds into desirable resources that institutions can "tap" to gain advantage (Michaels; Schroeder) or that students can use to sell themselves in seeking employment (Engberg, "Educating"; Jayakumar; Urciuoli, "Skills"). As something owned by individuals who have particular differences, diversity is also something that can be possessed by institutions that accumulate diverse individuals. In this way, diversity helps institutions enhance their pedigrees and the value of their degrees in a global (but not local or domestic) marketplace.[2]

This diversity talk is related to more than how universities market themselves to prospective students. In adopting market behaviors, Sheila Slaughter and Gary Rhoades argue, schools "also market their students. Many regard their student bodies as negotiable, to be traded with corporations for external resources. . . . When students graduate, colleges and universities present them to employers as output/product, a contribution to the new economy, and simultaneously define students as alumni and potential donors" (327). So at the same time that institutions recruit students, they orient to those students as if they are raw materials that can enhance the educational products they are "selling." These market logics are deeply embedded within Midwestern's diversity discourses.

Unfortunately, in the same way that Midwestern's diversity rhetorics articulate value for "targeted ethnic groups" and frame such targeted group members as "resources" that can be "tapped" in order to enrich the education that students are buying, individual student bodies are also assigned value. A powerful illustration of this diversity market appears in Catherine Prendergast and Nancy Abelmann's critique of metaphors of kinship and diversity in higher education. Prendergast and Abelmann show that the problem of orienting to student bodies in terms of value is that not all bodies are valued in the same ways, and portraying the benefits of diversity in a manner that obscures differences in how different bodies experience that diversity may only reinforce the status quo that universities like MU seek to change.

Within the MUDA and in Midwestern's diversity rhetoric, "diverse" bodies—from targeted groups—are valuable because they add diversity to the school. Admissions policies also accord value to student bodies with experiences overcoming adversity, alumni parents, and unique talents, including musical or athletic ability. But outside the school, in the "global workforce" that students are being trained to enter, market values shift dramatically for students from targeted ethnic groups. And here lies a very real tension between valuing material goods and valuing cultures and backgrounds. Christopher Newfield explains, "The university is in general not-for-profit, meaning that it exists to *spend* money on making citizens, engineers, writers, and the other forms of what is sometimes called 'human capital' and that can also be called the creative capability of always-evolving society" (169). In other words, the value of an academic field of study is not reducible to its ability to generate income or develop a salable product. Nor can students' bodies be valued solely based on their future earning potential (Prendergast and Abelmann) or the potential economic benefit they might bring the university (Schroeder). However, this is precisely what neoliberal discourses do with diversity: they define diversity based on its ability to enhance individuals' and institutions' market values.

The danger of applying a neoliberal frame to student bodies is particularly well illustrated in Prendergast and Abelmann's discussion of a website called "MyRichUncle." Now defunct, "MyRichUncle" at one time purported to help students without wealthy families to finance their education by matching them up with "Rich Uncles" who would sponsor students' education and, in return, receive the promise of being repaid with a percentage of the students' earnings after graduation. While advertised as a neutral market mechanism for helping students afford college, "MyRichUncle" instead made patently clear the different values accorded to different student bodies. Potential "Rich Uncles" use their knowledge of students' earning potential to determine which students they will sponsor. Thus, as Prendergast and Abelmann note, "through the objective instrument of the marketplace, white alumni will choose their fictive white kin to invest in, not because they are 'white,' but because they are worth more" (46)—that is, White students are likely to make more money upon graduation. Moreover, the emphasis on global markets for diversity, as illustrated in Midwestern's diversity rhetoric, renders less valuable "people of color with domestic genealogies" (Prendergast and Abelmann 49). In this situation, too, White students are poised to benefit from "diverse" educational environments because such contexts heighten their marketability in claiming valued cross-cultural competencies. Empirical research shows that such skills are in fact enhanced for White students who grew up in predominantly White communities and who matriculate at racially diverse colleges and universities (Jayakumar).

This tension between local and global is especially pointed in the way institutional appeals to diversity ignore the conflict between the cultural values of "targeted" student bodies and the student bodies that bear value in the global markets outside of the institution. At the same time that Midwestern examines its local community to consider which populations are underserved and underrepresented, it turns to global markets to explain the value of such diversity. But in global markets, it is international or global diversity that matters, not one's local community or background. By using neoliberal discourses to assign value to diversity and by obscuring the local and contextualized nature of many intergroup and cross-cultural interactions, such diversity discourses make it difficult to identify or alter systematic practices that legitimate oppression and disenfranchisement. Indeed, the way Midwestern frames its responsibility to cultivating difference emphasizes recruiting racially and ethnically diverse students who will make the university more marketable.

DIVERSITY AS PROPERTY

Students' marketability is ascribed on the basis of their race–ethnic category membership—or, as sociologist Lisa Wade suggests, by their ability to visibly represent race–ethnic diversity. Emphasizing diversity in terms of visible representations of race and ethnicity or through membership in particular race–ethnic categories can exacerbate the commodification of "diverse" student bodies when those categories are treated as stable, objectively real things that persist across time, rather than as historically and locally situated human creations. To acknowledge that identity categories are created is not to say they are fictions; it is to resist the fixity that is sometimes implied by institutional race–ethnic categorizations. By classifying people in particular ways, the race–ethnic categorizations MU uses have consequences for how students, faculty, and staff see themselves and others.

A pair of examples highlights two common ways that people are defined within institutional race–ethnic categorization systems. In the first example, a student straddles two choices presented to her on a demographic survey, and in the second, a student protests a broad category's erasure of a more specific identity. Both examples expose a gap between institutional language for difference and the everyday experiences in which people negotiate their identities.

I asked the students in the classroom I studied to complete a written demographic survey. The survey's questions were culled from terms used by Midwestern University in annual reports prepared by its Office of Institutional Research, as well as from categories prevalent in talk about first-year students and postsecondary students more generally (e.g., Penrose; Tinto). Because the categories on my demographic survey were used for many purposes across campus, I expected them to be familiar to students. And yet, when I first administered this questionnaire during a pilot study, one student raised her hand and asked me whether I wanted her to circle "Foreign" or "Asian/Pacific Islander" on the "Ethnic/Racial Background" question.

A bit surprised by the student's question and uncomfortable telling her how to answer, I told her to respond as if she were completing a university form. Later, as I reflected on that exchange, I realized that all I had done was shift the definition of terms away from what I wanted toward what the university wanted. But in neither case was she asked to assert her own self-identification. In other words, the "Ethnic/Racial Background" question does not ask how she sees herself; it asks how she should be classified by the institution. By requiring students to participate in particular systems of naming, institutional discourses shape students' self- and other-perceptions.

The question about students' "Ethnic/Racial Heritage" on MU's 2003–04 application for undergraduate admissions lists six possible options: "African American/Black"; "American Indian or Alaska Native / Tribal Affiliation: _____"; "Southeast Asian: Cambodian, Hmong, Laotian, Vietnamese"; "Other Asian/Pacific Islander"; "Hispanic/Latino"; "White/Non-Hispanic."[3] These categories are in part mandated by the federal Office for Management and Budget (OMB), although MU diverges from the OMB categories in distinguishing between "Southeast Asian" and "Other Asian/Pacific Islander." There are, of course, many other ways to identify people; these six categories are not the only race–ethnic categories by which people can be classified. As a relatively simple category system, these six race–ethnic categories evince a great deal of what public policy scholar Dvora Yanow calls "categorical lumpiness," subsuming multiple ways of identifying underneath a single term. The presentation of these six options implies that group membership is straightforward and unproblematic: one either is, or is not, a member of a particular category, an assumption clearly challenged by the student unsure which choice she should select.

Not only are individuals relegated to only one identity category (the 2003–04 question explicitly instructed, "Check one box," although the 2011–12 application allowed students to select multiple races), but also differences between members of any given category are erased. In spite of the descriptive limitations of a broad category name, these classifications remain deeply important in contemporary US society, not least because perceptions of and orientations to race and ethnicity have real consequences. Nevertheless, it is important to critically examine how classification systems perpetuate particular ways of organizing people. While providing students with a set of six category options is perhaps a more efficient way to construct diversity than allowing students to self-identify, it also means that students are incorporated into a race–ethnic category system defined by the institution. This move heightens the potential for what Schroeder calls institutional misrepresentation, a phenomenon the Proyecto Pa'Lante students he worked with encountered as they found "their experiences and expertise reduced to binary terms" (100).

The discrepancy between the generality of "lumpy" institutional category systems and the particularity of individual experiences is pointedly illustrated as an Indian American college student describes at length how an "Asian" category erases a more specific "Indian" identity:

> What really bothers me is when it comes to politically correct labeling. We're from Asia. India is in Asia, quite obviously in Asia. But Asian Americans and all my Oriental/Pacific Rim friends, or whatever you want to say, they're all, "You're Asian American?" Yeah, I am. India is very obviously in Asia, look at the map. But it's not when you say Pacific Rim. Or you could say Southeast Asian, but they think that's wrong, but we are considered Southeast Asian. But they're like, "No, that's Thailand, Cambodia, and Laos." So they've come up with "subcontinental," which I think is most horrible. I'd say I'm Asian,

but people are going to think Asian is what you look like. They're going to think automatically [that] an Asian person looks Japanese or Chinese, not look Indian. They think we're Middle Eastern. We're not Middle Eastern, we're Asian. (qtd. in Ortiz and Santos 62–63)

This student's comment shows how assumptions about what a particular category means can obscure or exclude other nonstandard definitions. As Yanow writes, "Every time we use a category name that lumps together several identities, we enforce the characteristics of that lumpier identity in its limited range on those subsumed under the name" (215). This erasure is one outcome of the institution's reliance on a limited category scheme and the consequent distribution of that category scheme across campus.

These two examples show college students trying to locate themselves within limited institutional classification systems, and both cases point to ways that classifications matter to students. While the dynamism of lived experience is difficult to fit into a restricted set of category descriptors, there are practical reasons that motivate institutions' use of such systems. For one thing, it is much easier to manage a small set of categories than an unwieldy list including all the ways that people might name themselves. For another, consistency in categories allows those categories to be compared over a period of time. Institutional categories thus serve the purpose of making differences quantifiable—that is, trackable and measurable. MU officials make this point in a 2011 "Diversity Report" that they preface with the following disclaimer: "This presentation is limited to variables for which we have quantitative information, including race/ethnicity, income level, first-generation in college, gender, and geographic diversity. Information is not systematically available for other groups that are important to inclusive excellence." The message is clear: even though other factors may matter, in order to count, differences must be countable. But by naming and abstracting particular types of differences, category systems also reify the differences they count, converting them from rich and dynamic facets of individuals' lived experiences into measurable variables.

Category stability is only illusory, however. Category names are always changing and are often used in inconsistent ways. At MU, for example, multiple names are used for single ethnic groups, such as "Native American" in the university's annual data release and "American Indian" through the registrar's office. Changes in federal guidelines for reporting race and ethnicity have also led to revisions to MU's data tracking ("Information for Users of Student Race/Ethnicity Data"). But these changes are rarely remarked upon or explained, and the categories themselves are treated as enduring and stable concepts. This reification obscures the ways that identity categories are socially constructed, as well as any understanding of how their historical emergence might matter for contemporary situations (see, e.g., D. Miller). Such forgetting is natural, according to Yanow: "Coming to perceive an external, objective reality in collective, human constructions, and then forgetting its artifactual origins, is the very process of constructing the social world" (208). However, this process also masks the potential for human actors to change or impact the images and categories disseminated by "the state" or "the institution."

The proliferation and distribution of these categories on college campuses, and in particular at MU, are not neutral acts; they are consequential for the way individuals negotiate those environments. As Kerry Ann Rockquemore and David Brunsma's study of multiracial identity reveals, simple race–ethnic classification systems show little of the range and variation within categories, and debates regarding multiracial identities and the US census (see Rockquemore and Brunsma; Williams; Yanow) have emphasized that such classifications are increasingly out of touch with the ways that everyday people make use of race–ethnic designations to understand themselves. Therefore, it is important to attend to how people organize themselves—institutionally *and* interactionally— and not to take these modes of organization as natural or given.

As race and ethnicity have come to be reified in talk about diversity, institutional systems for tracking membership in race–ethnic categories have oriented to differences as things to be counted and measured. The emphasis is not on ways that people talk and interact around difference but on the visible and measurable representation of difference on the MU campus. Such systems presume stability and (relative) permanence, and do not showcase the fluctuations and change that characterize everyday interactions with others. When channeled through discourses of neoliberalism proliferating at today's universities, such race–ethnic tracking converts individual features into commodities that can be bought, traded, and sold within diversity markets.

DEFINING DIVERSITY

One place where people have responded to the limitations of a simple race–ethnic category system is by defining diversity as encompassing all kinds of differences, not solely those of race and ethnicity. At MU, definitions of diversity often take such an expansive approach. Consider the following definition taken from an MU website titled "Diversity in Admissions":

> [Midwestern University] defines diversity broadly, to include and acknowledge differing personal characteristics and talents as well as social and cultural differences due to gender, race, ethnicity, socioeconomic status, age, nationality, religion, physical ability, and sexual orientation. As educators we value a breadth of perspectives as essential to the sifting and winnowing of the search for truth. The educational benefits of enhanced diversity will
>
> - enrich the educational experience and promote student learning;
> - foster cross-cultural understanding and a respect for differences;
> - enhance access and opportunity for all; and
> - prepare citizens and leaders for the global community.

This definition identifies numerous traits and emphasizes them all as important to diversity. Other diversity definitions make similar claims regarding the range of differences under the rubric of diversity. An epigraph to the MUDA reads: "Diversity of viewpoints, diversity of backgrounds, including gender and ethnic differences, as well as variety within academic specialties, are all vital components of the intellectual life of this great University." Here again, *diversity* includes, but is not limited to, race and ethnic diversity.

Using *diversity* as an umbrella term for a wide range of differences is a common way to define it. In her ethnographic study of a small liberal arts college, Urciuoli traces the school's shift from using the words *multicultural* and *multiculturalism* to using *diverse* and *diversity*. According to Urciuoli, this shift came about in part because *diversity* was more semantically flexible: *multicultural* was too intertwined with race and ethnicity ("Excellence"). Treating *diversity* as a broadly inclusive term is also prevalent in mainstream talk about diversity. In a series of interviews with everyday people about what diversity meant to them, sociologists Joyce Bell and Douglas Hartmann found that participants typically offered descriptions of diversity that encompassed a variety of differences. However, when asked to offer examples of diversity in their daily lives, almost all of the interviewees turned to race and ethnicity as illustrations.

A similar move is made by MU, as official definitions emphasize the breadth encompassed by diversity while at the same time tracking diversity by measuring race and ethnic category membership. Consider the distinction between the range of data that MU tracks in an "Annual Data Release" and the narrower data employed to measure progress on diversity goals. The "Annual Data Release" publishes official university statistics, and the information about students contained in this release includes gender, age, race/ethnicity, state of residency, major, and academic preparation as measured by high school rank and standardized test scores. While the "Annual Data Release" provides a general demographic sketch of enrolled students, progress on five of the MUDA's "Seven Core Goals" is measured by counting the number of students from four "targeted ethnic groups" who enroll, are retained, and graduate, as well as the number of faculty and staff from the same underrepresented groups who are hired and promoted. (The other two goals address increasing financial aid for "needy students" and building accountability measures for diversity.)

These four targeted ethnic groups (sometimes referred to as "targeted minorities") have been the near-exclusive focus of MU's diversity efforts since the early 1990s, although some recently articulated diversity goals focus on "needy students" (MUDA) and increasing the representation of "women in the STEM areas" ("Updated Diversity Plan"). To point out MU's focus on race and ethnicity is not to say that other categories are unimportant. Nor is it to say that MU ignores these categories. Rather, it is to highlight the different ways that diversity definitions and (ac)counts of diversity work. This discrepancy is not inherently problematic, but it is important to openly acknowledge the ways that broadly inclusive definitions of diversity are supported by close attention to increasing the representation of underrepresented race–ethnic categories on campus. For example, while higher education researchers have linked race–ethnic representation and other diversity measures (such as diversity in perspective or socioeconomic background), making such links more visible in campus diversity discourse might also entail developing more flexible and nuanced ways of tracking race–ethnic membership (see, e.g., K. Brown).

Pursuing an increased representation of underrepresented students—what social psychologist Patricia Gurin and colleagues (Gurin, Dey, Hurtado, and Gurin) call "structural diversity" (in contrast to interactional diversity and classroom diversity, which are more fully discussed in Chapter 3)—is important. Increasing the representation of underrepresented students, faculty, and staff also increases opportunities for intergroup contact, heightens interest in different course offerings, and enables the sharing of divergent opinions and worldviews both inside and outside the classroom (see, e.g., Chang; Chang, Denson, Sáenz, and Misa; Milem; Smith). However, by focusing on diversity as something that can be quantified, measured, and tracked, structural diversity also orients to race–ethnic category membership as something that people and institutions can own: individuals are diverse by virtue of having particular race–ethnic identifications, and schools can accumulate diversity by recruiting diverse individuals. If Sandel and others are right in arguing that turning higher education into a market is also changing the fundamental nature of higher education, the same can be said about its effects on diversity. Orienting to students in terms of their economic value is problematic not only because it commodifies them but also because it contributes to a way of imagining the institution that subverts attention to issues of social justice and inequity.

WHO'S WHO IN DIVERSITY DISCOURSES?

Diversity discourses do not make arguments only about what counts as diversity; they also shape an image of the institution and ascribe different roles to various actors. One way that such work is done is through the rhetoric of "targeted ethnic groups" or "targeted minorities." This phrasing pervades the MUDA and persists in contemporary diversity discourses at MU; it also serves as an emblem for the way diversity actors are represented. A close analysis of the MUDA introduction reveals "targeted" groups as passive victims of discrimination and nontargeted groups as people who need to take action on behalf of diversity.

Composed by a Diversity Agenda Committee, the MUDA introduction reaches out to members of the MU campus and surrounding community to recruit their participation in working toward and achieving MU's diversity goals. The introduction speaks to a broad audience, including students, faculty, staff, alumni, university leaders, and members of the business community, urging "everyone" to work together to achieve diversity goals. Much of the introduction is given over to describing what has been done, what is currently being done, and what needs to be done on behalf of diversity. In naming these actions, first-person pronouns (*we, us, ourselves, our*) are prominent, appearing fifty-five times in the introduction's forty-five sentences. *We* occurs thirty-seven times and *us, our,* and *ourselves* occur eighteen times. However, these pronouns are used inconsistently, and each use invites questions about who is implicated in any particular *we, our,* or *us.* Despite the inconsistent pronoun referents, a persistent us–them relationship does take shape.

To understand how this relationship is formed, take a closer look at these pronouns. While sometimes *we* seems to be broadly inclusive, invoking every person at Midwestern, other times it is attached to specific actions taken on the part of the Diversity Agenda Committee. Each *we* in the document was coded as inclusive or restrictive. An inclusive *we* invokes everybody on campus, or at least suggests that the action named should be taken or perceived as having been taken on the part of everyone. A restrictive *we* refers to actions taken only by a specific group or set of individuals. *Our, ourselves,* and *us* were also included in the coding. Of the fifty-five occurrences of these pronouns in the MUDA introduction, sixty-three were coded as inclusive and thirty-six as restrictive (see Table 1.1). The total is greater than the sum because some pronouns were coded in more than one way.

Table 1.1: Inclusive/Restrictive First-Person Pronoun Coding

Inclusive 1	We = The institution of Midwestern University	44
Inclusive 2	We = Every person at Midwestern University	19
Restrictive 1	We = Midwestern University Diversity Agenda Committee members	35
Restrictive 2	We = Specific individuals or groups speaking for/on behalf of Midwestern University	1

The significance of this inclusive and restrictive coding is illustrated in the opening sentences of the MUDA introduction, represented in Table 1.2. In these sentences, *we*s that are broadly inclusive bookend *we*s that are restrictive. What results is a reading that opens and concludes with invitations for broad identification from "everyone" to share in diversity efforts even while it highlights the actions and contributions of a specific group, emphasizing the distinction between *we*s who take leadership and *we*s who are being told what they need to do. The sentences analyzed in Table 1.2 appear under a heading titled "Commitment," and each personal pronoun is highlighted: inclusive *we*s are surrounded by a solid box, ambiguous *we*s are surrounded with broken lines, and restrictive *we*s are highlighted in gray.

Table 1.2: Opening Sentences of the MUDA Introduction

1	[We] at [Midwestern University] have a tradition on which to build [our] continuing efforts to achieve a more diverse and welcoming campus.
2	In particular [we] have made real progress in the past ten years, stimulated by the 1988 [Midwestern Plan], the umbrella [State Postsecondary Network Impetus for Diversity], and the 1993 [Midwestern Engagement].
3	In creating this plan as part of the [Midwestern State Network Diversity Agenda], we have taken stock of what [we] have accomplished and have tried to analyze what [we] need to do differently in the coming ten years.
4	Our conclusion is that the commitment of people will make the biggest difference.
5	[We] have leadership and commitment from the [Midwestern University Regents] and President [M——], and from [our] alumni and the [Midwestern] business community, all of whom recognize the need for [our] university to act vigorously to prepare students from all ethnic backgrounds to live and work in a racially and culturally diverse world.
6	[We] on this campus must now all commit [ourselves] to working steadily and speedily to achieve the goals of this plan.

Inclusive *we*s representing "everyone at Midwestern University" appear at the beginning and the end of this section, as shown in the solid boxes in the first and last sentences. In the first sentence, *we* is modified by the adjective clause "at Midwestern University," explicitly identifying all people at Midwestern, past and present, as having built the tradition upon which the current Diversity Agenda rests. Similarly, in the last sentence, *we* is modified by the prepositional phrase "on this campus," which once again points to all people at MU needing to make a commitment to the Diversity Agenda.

Unlike the inclusive *we*s that frame this section, *we* is more ambiguous in the second and fifth sentences. For instance, in the second sentence, who has made progress? Everybody at Midwestern? Midwestern as an institution? A specific committee or group of people at Midwestern who have been involved in forming and implementing these diversity initiatives? Because of this confusion, the *we* that has made progress does not necessarily evoke all members of the MU community, although that is one possible interpretation. The *we* in the second sentence has been "stimulated" by three previous Diversity Agendas. While these agendas constitute part of an institutional history, it is a history that many at MU may not be familiar with. Consequently the *we* that has been stimulated more narrowly evokes a group of people who are purposefully building on previous initiatives. There is also a more inclusive interpretation of this *we,* in which it is understood as "the institution of Midwestern University." This interpretation indirectly references all members of the campus community. The *we* in the fifth sentence is similarly ambiguous. The phrase "we have leadership" can be construed on several levels, with the people specifically named providing leadership to the institution as a whole, to the community of people at Midwestern, and/or to the committee charged with "taking stock," "analyzing," and "concluding" what needs to be done. It remains unclear, though, whether all people at MU are following this leadership or whether this *we* references a specific set of individuals at Midwestern who have regular contact with those leaders.

In contrast to the inclusive or ambiguous *we*s in the first, second, fifth, and sixth sentences, a clearly restricted *we* appears in the third sentence and is implied in the fourth. These pronouns are highlighted in gray. *We* in the third sentence has performed specific actions related to the Diversity Agenda: "have taken stock" and "have tried to analyze." The *we* that has "taken stock" points to the members of the Diversity Agenda Committee since not all members of the campus community have "taken stock" or "tried to analyze" diversity at Midwestern. However, the *we* that has "accomplished" and who needs to do things differently can be both broadly and narrowly construed. The specificity of the opening *we* in the third sentence makes more complicated the work of untangling whether all members of the campus community are implicated in having accomplished things. In the fourth sentence, the possessive pronoun *our* in front of *conclusion* also points to a specific group of people who drew this conclusion, presumably the same people who in the third sentence "took stock" and "analyzed."

The ambiguity surrounding these first-person pronouns and the actors whom those pronouns index makes it difficult for readers of the document to fully identify with the actions presented within the text, even when, as in the section's opening and concluding sentences, the use of *we* clearly invites all members of the MU campus to align with the actions taken by the Diversity Agenda Committee. The positioning of inclusive *we*s thus frames the actions of specific *we*s on campus, and this parallelism offers one way that, despite the confusion of *we*s, the entire campus is still seemingly implicated in this work.[4] The ambiguity of *we*s also reinforces the distinction between a *we* who is taking leadership and a *we* who is being told how to work toward diversity.

While much of the MUDA introduction follows this opening section in its use of first-person pronouns that create and communicate an imagined version of the university comprising a collective *we* who is taking action on behalf of diversity, one section stands out because these personal pronouns disappear altogether. In a section titled "Goals," the MUDA authors provide an overview of the agenda's central aims, identifying three general goals related to diversity. The entire section is reprinted below:

Goals

The actions recommended in the [Midwestern University Diversity Agenda] are to achieve the goals of significantly improving the representation and academic success of members of four targeted ethnic groups, namely, American Indian, African-American, Latino/a, and Southeast Asian-American, among the student body, the faculty, and the staff; to improve the classroom and social climate of this campus for those groups; and to increase the depth of understanding by the large majority of us who are not in those groups for their values, customs, and experiences.

The passive constructions in this sentence distinguish it from others in the MUDA introduction. It opens with "The actions recommended in the [MUDA]," a phrase that masks both who is recommending as well as where these recommendations are coming from. Not only is the main clause of this sentence passive, but so too are all of the goals listed. Left unanswered is the question of who is expected to perform these actions: students, faculty, and staff? The entire Midwestern University community? The Diversity Agenda Committee?

To identify who is implicated in these goals, consider the recipients of the actions named here. The first two goals name actions designed to benefit the "four targeted ethnic groups" or "those groups." The third references a benefit for "the large majority of us who are not in those groups." Because legal decisions over affirmative action in higher education mandate that institutions explain the diversity rationale in terms of a broad benefit to an overall campus community and not as a specific benefit to particular groups, it is important to the agenda's authors to show that diversity has benefits for the entire Midwestern campus community, as well as to emphasize that "achieving our goals will benefit all students, faculty, and staff." And yet these benefits distinguish between targeted and nontargeted students, indicating that these groups will not share in the same benefits. What's more, "targeted ethnic group" students are frequently referenced in the MUDA, whereas nontargeted students ("White" and "Other Asian/Pacific Islander" students, according to the race–ethnic categories on the 2003–04 admissions application) are referenced only in opposition to targeted ethnic group students. More perplexing is the reference to "us" in this clause. Who is "us"? This final goal seems to imply that bringing "targeted ethnic group" students to campus will benefit a (mostly White) "majority of us" by enabling this majority to learn about other cultures and traditions.

The reference to "the majority of us" in the third benefit is the only reference to White students, faculty, and staff in the MUDA introduction, other than the naming of several White university leaders and Diversity Agenda Committee members. In fact, the only specific individuals and groups mentioned are the president of the entire Midwestern University system, the Board of Regents, and the state legislature (see Table 1.2), as well as "four targeted ethnic groups"—American Indian, African American, Latino/a, and Southeast Asian American. The MUDA introduction also mentions three "other groups in society who experience discrimination": "women in some fields; lesbian, gay, bisexual, and transgender persons; [and] disabled persons." Several other people and groups are quoted: an epigraph from a previous university leader, a definition of *diversity* attributed to the American Association of Colleges and Universities, and statements from four university leaders and diversity committee members. Thus, throughout this introduction, all the individuals and groups specifically named are either "leaders" or "discriminated against."

Even the collective nouns used to invoke entities at Midwestern University reinforce this dichotomy. *Groups* is the predominant generic term used, appearing fourteen times.[5] In eight of these instances, the word is modified by *ethnic,* as in "four targeted ethnic groups" or "the four ethnic groups," or even with *ethnic* left implicit, as in "the four groups." Of the other six references, *group* is preceded by *those,* as in "those groups" five times and once by *other.* That is, all but one instance of the word *groups* appearing in this document refer very specifically to American Indian, African American, Latino/a, and Southeast Asian American students, faculty, and staff. The sole exception is in the phrase "other groups in society who experience discrimination." At no point are White students mentioned or referenced.

Indeed, White students are implicit throughout the document only through their absence. For example, the phrase "the large majority of us who are not in those groups" indexes White students, but only because they are not in an "ethnic" group, perpetuating the invisibility of Whiteness as a salient racial characteristic. Moreover, referenced through the phrase "the majority of us," White students are framed as already part of the institution, while non-White students are something of an anomaly, something strange and different that will be of interest—and benefit—to those already on campus. The students who are imagined as already belonging to the institution can be understood in terms of what Mitchell L. Stevens calls the "typical student." According to Stevens, even as colleges aggressively recruit multicultural students, the "typical student" remains their "bread and butter" (177). The changes in his college's enrollment of students of color are marginal, he argues, because it continues to pursue "most of its business on the presumption that its primary clientele would continue to be typical students" (178–79). In this way, imagining the institution as comprising mainly "typical students" can prevent attention to ways that the campus community, organization, and climate explicitly cater to these unnamed and unmentioned yet ever-present groups.

This analysis reveals clear distinctions between who is named and who is not and between who does things and who has things done to them. These distinctions present the institution as already including some groups while framing other groups as desired and desirable entities who need to be included. When this distinction is considered alongside the tendency to explain the importance of diversity by articulating its market value, the resulting commodification of student bodies exacerbates the separation between White students and "targeted ethnic group" students.

To challenge the commodification of student bodies forwarded in the MUDA and to resist an imagined version of the university that constructs White students as already belonging and students of color as needing to be incorporated, we might further examine the actions people are asked to take on behalf of diversity. At Midwestern, students are framed as the primary implementers of diversity, but not all students are invited in equal ways to be agentive in doing this work. For instance, White students are cast as needing to be more active in diversity efforts, while underrepresented students are treated as if their primary role is to provide White students with the opportunity to learn about cultural difference. A second role targeted students play in these discourses is to be "discriminated against." In this role, underrepresented campus populations serve as a reminder to non-discriminated-against people of the need to work for social justice, to enact a kind of noblesse oblige to help those "who still suffer the social, economic, and educational consequences of discrimination" (MUDA, Introduction).

Some of these diversity discourses aim to persuade skeptics that diversity does impact them in positive ways and that consequently they should embrace institutional diversity measures. But it is troubling that the benefits of diversity for these skeptics are clearly distinct from the benefits for "targeted ethnic group" students, faculty, and staff. The result is language that includes and excludes different groups of people at different points. Furthermore, the emphasis on recruiting diverse student bodies that pervades MU's diversity discourses has not (yet) been paired with a deep or sustained attention to fostering processes of engaging one another in productive discourse (Duffy, "Virtuous"; Hoang), and it is precisely to such interaction that the rest of this book turns. Understanding how difference is being engaged by the people who breathe life into institutions means focusing on interpersonal spaces in which differences are taken up among participants. Such work can enable us to see differences as dynamic rather than as static entities, as relations between people rather than as individual traits, and as interactionally emergent, not as properties that can be bought, transferred, or sold.

2

Marking Difference: The Emergence of Difference as an Interactional Phenomenon

BECAUSE WRITING CLASSROOMS, ESPECIALLY FIRST-YEAR composition courses, reach students with a broad range of backgrounds, interests, and experiences, those classrooms also represent an ever-shifting terrain upon which differences of all kinds play out. Within the writing classroom, as students from across the curriculum come together, difference does not manifest as an individual property that people carry with them and wield as they interact with others. Instead, differences take shape as people come to know who they are in relation to others. Therefore, one central aspect of writing pedagogy involves teachers "coming-to-know" students in the writing classroom. This is not an easy task. "At the very most," Julie Lindquist writes,

> the project of "knowing" students entails knowledge about their histories, social situations, cultural backgrounds, class positions, material situations, learning styles, affective predicaments, and psychic states. At the very least, it means understanding *enough* about students' experiences as literacy learners and users to be able to infer what is at stake for them in pedagogical transactions of various kinds. ("What's" 175–76)

Lindquist's claim that knowing students is neither simple nor easily accomplished is reinforced by decades of writing research explicitly aimed at more deeply and comprehensively understanding students. Longitudinal studies of college teachers and students (e.g., Beaufort; Carroll; Fishman, Lunsford, McGregor, and Otuteye; Fishman and McCarthy; Herrington and Curtis; Sternglass) as well as ethnographic studies of literacy (e.g., Duffy, *Writing*; Heath; Hull and Schultz; Purcell-Gates) have generated richly nuanced insights about many different kinds of writers and their literacy practices. But no matter how rich, detailed, or groundbreaking this research, it does not cover all the situations, contexts, environments, and positions writing teachers find themselves in, nor all the differences they encounter in the classroom. Moreover, few writing teachers are well positioned to perform their own longitudinal studies or to follow students into their home communities and environments.[1] Yet the act of teaching involves an ongoing project of engaging the many student writers they encounter in their classrooms.

To help teachers make sense of this complex array of experiences, behaviors, and ways of being, this chapter offers a theory of difference as dynamic, relational, and emergent. This presentation of difference treats it as a rhetorical performance; in so doing, it resituates the problem away from *learning about*, and thus needing to know students, toward *learning with*, and thus always coming-to-know students. As its name implies, coming-to-know is a never-ending process, not a fixed destination; teachers never arrive at a place where they *know* a student. When teachers learn with their students, they situate what they know from personal experience and professional training alongside interpersonal interactions that enrich, complicate, and challenge those forms of knowing. And, while writing teachers generally realize they cannot assume that the students in front of them are exactly like other students they know personally or have encountered in the scholarly literature, such comparisons remain a central strategy for responding to issues of difference in classrooms. To avoid this difference fixation, this chapter outlines an orientation to difference as rhetorically negotiated through a process named here as "marking difference." When marking difference, rhetors and audiences alike display and respond to markers of difference, those rhetorical cues that signal the presence of difference between two or more participants.

Attention to marking difference and to categorization processes can help us identify and respond to difference as it emerges interactionally in our classrooms. The project of coming-to-know someone in the writing classroom entails an openness to how students mark themselves and us, as well as how we mark ourselves and our students. Such a stance can enable collaboration with students in processes of learning *with*, rather than learning *about*. While learning about and learning with complement one another in many ways, they also diverge in two important respects. First, learning about can privilege traditional discourses of power, such as published scholarship or teachers' prior knowledge, whereas learning with seeks to position teachers and students as co-participants in ongoing processes of knowledge construction, although power asymmetries remain.[2] Second, learning about focuses on the *what* of selves and others, on naming and describing difference, rather than on *how* selves and others move together in shared social space. Focusing on *how* people move underscores an orientation to difference as a rhetorical process of engagement as individuals position themselves in particular ways for particular purposes.

Examining how differences are performed in writing classrooms involves attention to how people rhetorically negotiate those spaces, but orienting to difference and sameness is difficult. Krista Ratcliffe names some of these challenges as she discusses a process of "non-identification" in which speakers and audiences are called to recognize a space of not-knowing, where "people recognize the partiality of [their] visions and listen for that-which-cannot-be-seen, even if it cannot yet be heard" (73). But how does one perform such listening? It may seem paradoxical to suggest that we can listen for what we cannot hear, yet this is precisely what the act of teaching in the face of difference entails: because we *cannot* fully know all of our students, we instead interact with them in a continual process of coming-to-know. In coming-to-know students, we do not begin with a blank slate, however; we all have prior experiences and training that inform how we orient to particular students and how we engage in processes of coming-to-know them. The stakes in these processes are high, a point made clear by the stories of mishearing and misunderstanding that pervade educational literature (see, e.g., Delpit; Pollock, *Everyday*; TuSmith and Reddy; Winkle-Wagner).

To illustrate the challenges and the risks inherent to processes of coming-to-know students in the writing classroom, I turn to

Ann Jurecic's descriptions of her work with a student in her class with whom she was unable to identify. Jurecic's efforts serve as a cautionary tale regarding the difference fixation. Her story also highlights some of the ethical dilemmas we face in our work with students. In the introduction, we saw how Charlie talked about his quiet students, wondering whether they were less confident as writers or students. Pervasive stereotypes about silence, reticence, and/or shyness likely influenced Charlie's orientations to and portrayals of quietness in his classroom. Various categories of difference, particularly those that are widely identified, are subject to different stereotypes and cultural representations. As a result, many of us consciously work to avoid essentializing these categories in our interactions with students. For some categories of difference, however, there are relatively few widely available or easily identified resources for thinking about and orienting to those categories in rich and productive ways. Disability is one such category.[3]

Attention to disability in the composition classroom is complicated by problematic discourses about disability that are part of everyday talk. In many ways, the narrative Jurecic tells is one of an individual teacher who "fixes" difference and "others" disability. But in other ways, Jurecic's story is a common one: the same writing research and training that regularly urge teachers to carefully orient toward, say, quiet students or toward race, gender, or class in the writing classroom less regularly and explicitly urge attention to disability as difference. This gap is where Jurecic tries to enter the conversation.

In its essence, Jurecic's pedagogical narrative is an attempt to answer the question, "What can teachers do when confronted with radical difference, difference that they either cannot or will not understand or identify with?" Her account shows the difference fixation at work: even as Jurecic pushes herself to find effective pedagogical approaches for working with Gregory, she demonstrates some of the risks of assuming knowledge about students. Ultimately, difference is never fully knowable, and teachers should not aim to *know* their students as much as willingly participate with them in processes of coming-to-know one another in the writing classroom. The discussion that follows summarizes Jurecic's description of her work with Gregory as she relates it in two different articles ("Mind-blindness," "Neurodiversity").

In both articles, Jurecic introduces Gregory by emphasizing his difference: "On the first day of class, Gregory stood out as different, even bizarre" ("Mindblindness" 1). She then details how Gregory's behavior was unorthodox and surprising to her and notes that she feels "off-balance" in communicating with him ("Mindblindness" 1). To find better ways of responding to him, she reaches out to others. She talks to a university administrator, during which conversation she learns that there is "no indication of any disorder or disability in Gregory's file" ("Neurodiversity" 425); she queries a neurologist; she reaches out to parents with autistic children; she identifies and talks with one of Gregory's high school English teachers; she reads scientific and medical research written by "autism experts" ("Neurodiversity" 425); she analyzes writing published by autistic people; she revisits writing research from the 1970s and 1980s on cognition and writing; and she engages recent research in cognitive science and neuroscience. These investigative efforts lead Jurecic to "diagnose" Gregory with Asperger's syndrome, a move in which she fixes Gregory's difference. While Jurecic seeks to fix difference, that is, to help students like Gregory and teachers working with students like Gregory to successfully negotiate encounters of this sort, she also fixes—that is, freezes—autism-as-difference by devoting considerable space in both essays to describing features and traits common to autistic people, even while acknowledging that there is great variation in the category. In performing what Margaret Price calls a "diagnostic treasure hunt" (55), Jurecic demonstrates her need to fix difference in order to respond to it in her classroom. When she "diagnoses" Gregory, some of his unique (or not-so-unique, depending on how you look at it) constellations of behaviors are brought together, solidified, known, and objectified under the categorical umbrella of Asperger's syndrome.

Largely absent from Jurecic's narrative of working with Gregory is, well, attention to her work with Gregory. Even though Jurecic presents a large repository of knowledge about autism and writing to argue that to better serve students with neurological disorders writing studies ought to forge stronger ties with science and medicine, a turn toward the classroom and the interactions within the classroom is just as warranted by what Jurecic reveals in her narrative. For us to come-to-know students like Gregory and how to work with them, we also need new ways of listening to our interactions with them. Gregory's perspective is absent from Jurecic's accounting. She claims that this is in part because she desires to preserve his anonymity and because talking about him in more than broad strokes would risk revealing his identity. But, as Amy Vidali points out, Jurecic here "communicates a troubling willingness to talk 'about' neurodiverse students with other academics and a distaste for having similar conversations with student subjects" (191): that is, Jurecic fixates on learning *about* Gregory rather than *with* him.

Indeed, the problem is not just the absence of Gregory's voice from Jurecic's accounts; it is also the way Jurecic talks about him. At the same time that she claims to value his intelligence and his abilities, she draws on cultural and scientific discourses about autism to paint a broad picture of "autistic people," and consequently of Gregory. He gets lost in a stereotypical portrait of autism that tells a story about what autistic people cannot do, a story that is largely drawn from literature on autism characterized by what John Duffy and Rebecca Dorner call "a rhetoric of scientific sadness" (202). Jurecic even replicates this rhetoric in her own work, as when she tries—and fails—to imagine what it would be like to be severely autistic.

Acts of imagining and empathy are powerful resources, but they are also limited, as critiques of performing disability simulations for the purpose of "learning what it is like" to have a particular disability reveal (French). In a similar vein, when teachers assume they know their students, they run the risk of enacting forms of over-identification that lead them to miss or ignore significant differences between themselves and their students. This is a phenomenon that Mary Louise Gomez, Anne Burda Walker, and Michelle L. Page observed as White, middle-class preservice teachers drew on their personal experiences to claim affiliation with the minority students they were mentoring; however, similar problems arise when teachers draw overly broad conclusions about particular types of students or apply "knowledge" unreflectively to individual students.

This is not to say that Jurecic's interest in and turn to other resources is inherently problematic: when confronted with unfamiliar situations or confusing pedagogical encounters, teachers often look for research that will help them move forward, sometimes looking to scholarship performed with particular student populations (such as ESL writers or basic writers), in particular pedagogical situations (one-to-one conferencing, peer review, managing classroom discussion), or between particular groups (men and women; interracial and interethnic encounters of all kinds). Teachers also turn to their colleagues for advice, as Lisa Gonsalves reports in her analysis of White faculty interactions with Black male students, and as several contributors to Bonnie TuSmith and Maureen Reddy's collection, *Race in the College Classroom,* assert. All of these resources can open up teachers' awareness of new categories and deepen insights about types of students and pedagogical practices. As a consequence of reading and engaging with this literature, teachers orient to students in new ways and with new vantage points.

However, despite the importance of such learning about particular groups, situations, and contexts, there remain risks, especially when such learning is not conversant with interpersonal encounters. When Jurecic "diagnoses" Gregory as having Asperger's syndrome, she uncritically privileges the powerful discourses of scholarly literature, science, Gregory's former teachers, and writing program administrators while ignoring less-powerful voices that are also playing a role in her interactions with Gregory. This is the effect of Jurecic's emphasis on medical discourses about autism while downplaying the importance of Gregory's own voice. Privileging some voices and not others is in some ways inevitable, as teachers everywhere invest in particular forms of knowledge as they make choices about what to do in their teaching. For instance, personal experiences and beliefs about what makes a classroom "safe" or about the value of particular kinds of writing will lead teachers to exclude or devalue some perspectives and beliefs. No teacher can hear everything; our experiences and knowledge dispose us to listen for particular voices and cues and not others. The asymmetries of listening always affect who and what will be heard, and it is hard to know what to listen for. So how can we listen for what we don't even know is there in the classroom? A strategy for flexible listening is one possibility.

To teach across a broad range of students, many of whom have backgrounds that are unfamiliar to us and all of whom have unique experiences that inform and shape their needs as learners, we need to cultivate practices of learning *with* our students, not just about them. As we look to identify what we don't know, we might also ask questions about *how* we know and about the ways that we and our students co-participate in processes of coming-to-know. To return to the example of Jurecic's discussion of Gregory, she primarily frames her task, and her contribution to writing pedagogy, as that of laying out the terrain of autism, rather than of highlighting the important work she does in "attend[ing] to how he responded to the class, the writing process, and [her] comments" ("Neurodiversity" 435). The pedagogical adaptations Jurecic makes in her classroom emerge from these acts of listening and responsiveness, not from the literature on autism.

Scholars working on autism and rhetoric have in fact challenged Jurecic's claim that working with autistic students necessitates learning about autism from a variety of popular and medical discourses. In "Autism and Rhetoric," Paul Heilker and Melanie Yergeau highlight ways that autism and autistic people have been problematically represented and go so far as to argue that "we might do best to unlearn everything we think we have learned about autistics, who, as a group, are about as amorphous and diverse as neurotypicals" (496). In other words, the answer they offer for working with autistic students is not a prescription, not a list of what to do, not a set of books and articles to read. Instead, Heilker and Yergeau write,

> If we can come to see our autistic students through the lens of rhetoric more than through a stock and overdetermined lens of autism, we might come to better appreciate what they do have to offer instead of fixating on what they do not. Indeed,

if we give them the opportunity, we might get a chance to learn how they see themselves. (496)

Marking difference provides a rhetorical stance that counteracts the overdetermined tale of autism told by Jurecic and contributes to the recovery of autism as rhetorical practice described by Heilker and Yergeau. This is not a rejection of the category of autism; it is a call to engage a dialectic between stasis and motion, between fixity and change. More can be done to understand how this dialectic is negotiated in the composition classroom. The next section outlines an approach to difference in which teachers actively cultivate awareness of new details, interpret and reinterpret those details, and contextualize them within specific moments of writing, teaching, and learning. This perspective offers a means for mediating between learning about broader categories and learning through classroom interaction.

MARKING DIFFERENCE: A WAY TO LISTEN

Broad identity categories are an integral part of the way we make sense of our lives. Even as these broad labels provide a necessary means for interpreting and understanding experience, they run the risk of stereotyping or misidentifying people. Literary scholar Michael Hames-García's discussion of the perils of essentialism emphasizes the danger of presuming too much sameness or unity within a group. The answer to this dilemma for some has been a turn to intersectionality, a rich consideration of how different factors shape identity and identifications. Intersectional understandings can be further enriched through attention to ongoing interactions for what they contribute to identity formation and interpersonal relationships.

Indeed, focusing on particular labels can sometimes constrain teachers' openness to various interpretive possibilities, as when Jurecic fixates on traits discussed in literature on autism to explain her work with Gregory. So what are teachers to do when students tell them, "I have Asperger's" or "I have autism"? According to Jurecic, students expect their teachers "not only to know what that means, but what to do" (Lewiecki-Wilson, Dolmage, Heilker, and Jurecic

324). But there is no simple answer to this question because there is no clear, consistent, or stable way of explaining what "I have autism" will mean for an individual student or for a teacher's working relationship with that student.[4] To be sure, I'm not saying that people should ignore their past experiences and professional training, nor am I suggesting that identity categories are meaningless constructs.[5] But I am saying that the answer to "what to do" resists prescription because of the dynamism, relationality, and emergence of difference. In what follows, I illustrate these features of difference by juxtaposing personal anecdotes from my experiences as a deaf academic and writing teacher alongside discussion of Mikhail Bakhtin's ethical scholarship.

I'm deaf. I'm also a White female, I wear glasses, and I grew up outside of Cleveland, Ohio. One could perhaps say that these are relatively static features of my identity: I wear glasses almost every waking hour, I've never *not* been White or female, I was born deaf, and I cannot change where I grew up. But at the same time, none of these features has a stable meaning. As I move in and out of different situations, some of them matter more at some times and less at others, and they take on different shades of meaning and nuance depending on who I am interacting with. That I wear glasses is inconsequential in most interactions, whereas the fact that I'm deaf matters significantly more often. But how these things matter is highly variable. Knowing these things about me will not tell you what you need to do when you meet me nor what adaptations you might make as you communicate with me. Knowing these things also doesn't determine how you will work with me as a student nor how I manage as a teacher in front of a classroom.

If you too are deaf, or if you've worked or lived with other deaf people, or if you've ever met a deaf person, or if you've read research by or about deaf people, or if you've seen representations of deaf people in popular media, you might be able to form some hypotheses about what I do in the classroom to accommodate my deafness. And the more experience you have with deaf people, the more you will likely come to realize the variation within that category, and the more you'll realize that you can't *know*—without meeting me, talking to me, or interacting with me in some way—exactly how my deafness matters and when it matters. When you meet me, you might find that I fit a lot of your assumptions about deaf people and that many of your predictions were accurate. But you might also find that I challenge or resist your expectations.

It is awkward for me when I encounter someone who either ignores or does not understand my cues about how best to communicate with me, whether I convey these cues indirectly (e.g., by moving myself physically so I can see the person's face) or by making direct requests (e.g., "Please talk to me, not to the interpreter"). When these scenarios happen, I have to decide whether I'm going to openly engage, whether I'll play along, or whether I'll simply try to extricate myself from the situation. For this reason, I find myself strongly disagreeing with Jurecic when she says that when teachers meet autistic students they should "know" not only "what that means, but what to do" (Lewiecki-Wilson et al. 324). I resist this claim largely because it is not true for me and the way I prefer people to approach me, but also because emphasizing what we know or should know leaves scant room for students and teachers to co-construct knowledge about what it means to work together in a classroom.[6] There is a real gap between what we (think we) know about types of students, pedagogy, and "what works" and the interactions we have in our classrooms that bring differences of all kinds alive.

To shift the emphasis toward ways of learning with our students rather than about them, I suggest we might benefit from paying close attention to how differences take shape within classroom interactions. From such a perspective, difference is not presentable through categories or static across time and space. Instead, it is dynamic, it is relational, and it is emergent in interaction. Teachers cannot study difference and respond to it by cataloging or even predicting all the potential differences that might affect their classroom or pedagogy. So what might happen if we learn to listen, as Katherine Schultz and Krista Ratcliffe have each urged us to do, to difference as it takes shape while people learn and write in a wide variety of social contexts?

To demonstrate how such an orientation to difference might be built, I draw on Bakhtin's ethical scholarship to show difference as dynamic, relational, and emergent—three qualities that are not always well represented in talk about difference in writing research. Within that theoretical lens, I develop the concept of markers of difference, contextually embedded rhetorical cues that signal the presence of difference between one or more interlocutors, and suggest that markers of difference can bridge the conceptual gap between knowledge about difference and interactional involvement with difference. Having a marker-based orientation to difference is important because when people write and read, they wrestle with not just texts but also selves. To read and respond to others involves making sense of the locations individuals occupy in relation to others, and doing such work requires a way of asking questions about how people are different from one another and what those differences mean.

In contrast to understanding difference as something to be named or described, I define difference as a relation between two individuals that is predicated upon their separateness from one another, or what Bakhtin refers to as noncoincidence in being (*Toward*). This relation is signaled by the display and uptake of markers of difference. Difference-as-relation drives communicative efforts because it is part of the interplay between identification and differentiation. This interplay reveals the lived experience of difference as highly dynamic. This dynamism is not always well articulated through broad category labels that draw coherence from their ability to move across contexts. Such labels can, in fact, suppress attention to the ways that individual actors display and respond to difference. Therefore, I want to suggest an approach focused on understanding the shaping of difference interactionally. Marking difference is a rhetorical lens—rhetorical because it emphasizes the relationship between speaker/writer and audience as well as the situated nature of all communicative activity—that acknowledges the important role identity categories play in interactions at the same time that it attends to difference as it is performed during the moment-to-moment vicissitudes of communication.

Because they foreground individual responsibility and the uniqueness of each act of communication, Bakhtin's early ethical writings in *Toward a Philosophy of the Act* and *Art and Answerability* are important to this understanding of difference. What Bakhtin calls the "once-occurrent event of Being" (*Toward* 2) can be understood in terms of the singularity of each rhetorical situation. No two individuals will ever have the same relation to each other as they do to any other individual, and no situation will be exactly like any other current, past, or future situation. Bakhtin's work also foregrounds individual activity, which he describes as "participatory" and "responsible." Individuals have a responsibility, he argues, to make the most of every moment. To accept this responsibility is to maintain an openness to the Other, to keep possibilities open rather than to close them off.

Bakhtin's conceptions of "the once-occurrent event of Being" and responsibility to the Other in communication highlight difference as dynamic, relational, and emergent. Difference is dynamic because meanings shift from moment to moment and are continually evolving. To return to the example of my deafness, when I encounter a student who doesn't realize I'm deaf and asks me about my accent, I am positioned very differently than I am by a student who does realize that I'm deaf and who asks me if I know sign language. In both cases, it may be the sound of my voice that marks me as different to these students, but each one takes up that marker in a different way and puts me in a different position to respond. In turn, as the conversations progress, the first student comes to realize that I'm not a foreigner and that I am deaf (shifting the meaning of the different-sounding voice), and the second student comes to realize that I may embody qualities that differentiate me from their expectations about deaf people. I, in my turn, choose to display particular cues in response—explaining that I'm deaf to the first student and saying aloud, "Yes, I do," to the second while not signing anything—in an attempt to assert my own claims about how I want to be identified and to shape our future interactions. In interaction, what any one marker may mean for individual identity and interactional possibility is always shifting. Markers point to that dynamism by highlighting how individuals can deploy different markers to challenge or modify previous ones.

In similar fashion, the meanings associated with identity categories shift over time, through subtle moment-by-moment changes in individuals' impressions of one another that occur in interaction. This is what Bakhtin describes as the "unfinishedness" of being. He writes, "I have to be, for myself, someone who is axiologically yet-to-be, someone who does not coincide with his already existing makeup" (*Art* 13). Every semester when I meet students for the first time, my students and I negotiate my deafness; even though such encounters are familiar to me, at the same time, no one semester beginning is identical to other semesters. I confess to once upon a time feeling a secret thrill when students would comment that at first they didn't realize I was deaf. Now, however, I always assert my deafness. I have learned—from repeated encounters of this sort—my preferred way of managing the situation. I am not the same person I was when I felt that excitement at "passing," and I never seem to answer questions about my deafness the same way twice. I am always yet-to-be, always moving toward a new position or awareness, using different tools and resources for managing my identity in these situations.

In being yet-to-be, individuals are never coincident even with themselves. They do not remain in the same place, and the differences they display and what those differences mean are always shifting. Part of the reason differences are always shifting is because difference is relational. No two individuals have the same relation to each other, and difference cannot be considered in isolation: it inherently implies a comparison. I am not different by virtue of my deafness any more than a hearing person is different because of his or her hearingness. I am different from other deaf people, and I am different from hearing people. While many aspects of self and Other cannot be fully articulated (or even apprehended by individuals themselves), it is with markers of difference that people create, display, and respond to changes in self and Other and the perceived relations between them. To acknowledge individuals' yet-to-be-ness is to maintain an openness to one's own and others' identities and to avoid treating identity markers as fixed or static elements.

Following from these principles of dynamism and relationality, difference is emergent. It does not exist outside of the interactional moment but, rather, takes shape as individuals make choices about what to reveal about themselves, what to notice or comment on—or to not notice or comment on. To communicate across difference, people must always be looking to learn what more they do not know about the Other; they must avoid presuming they can know the Other as a totalized and whole consciousness. It is insulting, for example, when people assume I cannot understand spoken discourse because I am deaf. To presume to know me is to close off interactional possibilities rather than to hold them open. Bakhtin describes the assumption of wholeness in terms of moments in which people step outside of themselves and enter into ("consummate") the Other (*Art*). But, just as students cannot literally enter my mind and "know" me, total consummation can never occur, because it would violate the uniqueness of every moment of being. Indeed, as mentioned previously, this uniqueness is such that people are never even coincident with themselves: I am always yet-to-be; I am always coming to know who I am. I cannot know every aspect of even my own identity and self. As Bakhtin writes, one's life "finds no rest within itself and never coincides with its given presently existing makeup" (*Art* 15).

Because markers are fleeting, often existing only in a single moment, they demand sensitivity to each moment. The ephemerality of markers helps balance the persistence of categories. Difference is not "out there" waiting to be found and identified but is always coming-to-be through the here-and-now of interaction. In the moment of interaction, engaging difference is a situated activity during which individuals consciously and unconsciously display markers of difference to distinguish between themselves and others. When someone decides to use a particular marker, that decision is cast against already existing ideas of how others may respond to that marker; people choose the markers they hope will best accomplish their interactional and relational goals. Not all markers are purposefully chosen, however. I can influence my raced and gendered appearance, for instance, but I cannot erase race and gender from my self-presentation entirely. I also cannot choose for other people what cues they will interpret, although the markers of difference that I choose to display are informed by what past experiences have taught me about negotiating similar or parallel situations.

In processes of coming to know the Other and coming to know the self, the relationality of difference comes into sharpest focus: only through interaction with Others are we able to apprehend ourselves. This awareness subsequently shapes our consciousness of the markers others are orienting to and how they take on meaning. This process is akin to what Bakhtin describes as "evaluat[ing] our exterior not for ourselves, but *for* others *through* others" (*Art* 33, Bakhtin's emphasis). Identities are always in flux, always yet-to-be, so they are never fully known or knowable entities, and knowledge about self comes only through encounters with Others. Encountering Others in the here-and-now gives individuals insight into their own selves. When I meet students who ask about my accent, I am reminded that I sound "different" from many hearing speakers when I talk, in a way that I am not when speaking with people who are already familiar with my speaking voice. By situating my own understanding against other people's, I am able to make predictions about how the markers I display will be taken up and responded to. The accuracy of my predictions changes over time, as I gain experience and familiarity in some contexts and move in and out of others. While I cannot completely alter my speaking voice to adapt to a particular situation, many times I do make a concerted effort to address any challenges that may be posed by my voice when I anticipate that someone will have difficulty understanding me. Taken together, these three elements—dynamism, relationality, and emergence—constitute a rhetorical presentation of difference in their emphasis on how individuals call attention to—or suppress—difference, as well as how they respond to differences displayed by others.

At this point, it will be helpful to distinguish my use of the word *marker* from another common use: to refer to objects or modes that are marked, such as a marked case in linguistics. The marked case is stressed and set apart from unmarked or otherwise unemphasized cases. For example, when Ruth Frankenberg talks about Whiteness as "a set of cultural practices that are usually unmarked and unnamed" and describes the task of her book as that of "exploring, mapping, and examining the terrain of whiteness" (1), she argues that there are salient features of Whiteness that can be identified (marked) even though they are not currently named and discussed. In this context, people may describe practices of "marking difference" that locate difference against an unstated norm, such as when someone might say that my deafness marks me as different. I do not use the term *marker* in this way. To evoke my deafness as difference, it must be considered relationally: How does my not-hearing (of a particular form) make me different from a specific interlocutor? Is this difference taken up by either participant? And if so, how does this marker of difference—whatever it is that cues my deafness or my interlocutor's relationship to my deafness—become salient for each of us?

Thus, in contrast to the way that a stance of learning about others may presume the significance of broad labels for interactional possibility, markers show difference as shaped through interaction. For something to be a marker of difference, it must be taken up in a communicative encounter. On its own, a marker has no stable meaning. This is one reason that markers of difference are so deeply rhetorical: they require involvement between a speaker/writer and an audience, and they must be located in their rhetorical context. Markers are used to point to and articulate difference, and some markers are readily engaged while other intended markers may be ignored, suppressed, or disregarded. Category labels can also be used as markers—names with which people mark themselves as, say, members of a particular group.[7] I do this when I describe myself as "deaf" (and sometimes as "profoundly deaf," although this more specialized term is only meaningful for particular audiences). It is a rhetorical choice: I do not say "hard-of-hearing" or "partially deaf" or "hearing-aid-wearer," although these terms are sometimes used by other people in talking about me. In this way, people use categorical terms to mark others as well as to assert their own identity claims. Markers of difference provide a mechanism for realizing the ephemerality of difference in interaction while also attending to broader representations and signifiers that influence what gets noticed and how meaning gets made in particular contexts.

Markers can be ascribed to people and interpreted off of their bodies and material possessions, as when people notice my hearing aids and form their own conclusions from that noticing. The physical accoutrements of identity, including clothing, accessories, and material objects, also act as markers of difference. An example will help show how clothing choices mark difference in both purposeful and unconscious ways. In college, I owned a T-shirt that featured a movie poster for the film *The Adventures of Ford Fairlane*, with the words "starring Andrew Dice Clay" written at the bottom of the shirt. I'd never seen the movie and I'd never heard of Andrew Dice Clay, but I thought the T-shirt was cool. One day an older friend of mine, with a look of consternation, asked me why I was wearing Andrew Dice Clay on my shirt. I shrugged and told her that I liked the picture on the shirt. She didn't say anything else. But the fact of her asking the question, along with her facial expression, signaled to me that there was *some* meaning of which I was probably unaware, so I looked him up and came to identify new ways that my shirt might be read by others. Becoming aware of other potential interpretations of my T-shirt led me to understand how my clothing choices might lead people to ascribe to me particular identity claims.[8]

Category identifications are always a part of interactional processes, so much so that for some categories people may explicitly solicit category identifications if group affiliation is not immediately perceivable. Gender, for example, is so central to interaction that many people do not know how to behave if they do not know an interlocutor's gender—a phenomenon that is humorously addressed in a series of *Saturday Night Live* skits focused on an ambiguously gendered character named "Pat" (see Ridgeway). Race and ethnicity are also highly visible and frequently marked identity categories (see Omi and Winant), but they are not always easily—or accurately—read off of a person's body, appearance, comportment, or dress.[9] Of particular interest to marking difference are unstable categories, such as disability, that are highly variable in their everyday manifestations (see Siebers, *Disability*).

Teachers and students are always engaging in processes of marking difference: they interpret purposeful and unconscious cues that others display, and they respond with cues of their own in which they position themselves and come-to-know ways in which they are similar to and different from one another. Identity categories are integral to processes of marking difference both as terms that people use to mark themselves and others and as ways that people cluster various markers to make sense of them. Table 2.1 provides an overview of questions that guide the two approaches to studying difference discussed here. These questions reinforce ways that analyses of difference are shaped by the underlying orientations to difference outlined earlier, learning about and learning with. The analyses that I perform in Chapters 3 and 4 focus on the second set of questions, emphasizing a perspective that works from participants' understandings of an interactional moment and centers on how their rhetorical choices respond to, constitute, and direct that moment.

Table 2.1: Questions for *Learning about* and *Learning with* Others

Learning About	Learning With
• What differences are present in the classroom? • What groups do individuals belong to? • What names or labels can describe particular individuals and/or associate them with others? • What can we learn about the individuals in the classroom? • What information about the self is being communicated in talk?	• How do individuals position themselves alongside others? • How are individuals positioned by others? • How do individuals acknowledge similarities and differences between themselves and others? • What differences are made salient through classroom interactions? • How are students and teachers learning with others in the classroom?

Both sets of questions in Table 2.1 invite us to better understand our students and our relationships with them. However, the first set, focused on learning about, prioritizes what we are already aware of as potentially significant and centers on patterns of noticing (and not-noticing) informed by context, situation, and setting. We use broad descriptions of this sort as we characterize our classes or talk about our students. While these descriptions can sometimes predict, they do not determine students' positions and relationships between themselves, their teachers, or their institutions (see, e.g., Sullivan and Nielsen). However, such predictive work is only useful insofar as we also have tools for revisiting or revising the meanings attributed to these representations. Markers of difference address this issue because the repeated noticing of particular markers of difference or particular styles of marking can cultivate sensitive and complex articulations of difference. In this way, with the second set of questions, markers of difference build reflexivity between our categorical awareness and the meanings we ascribe to those categories.

A TURN TOWARD ANSWERABLE ENGAGEMENT

How might an orientation to markers of difference and the questions in Table 2.1 provide guidance and insight for us as we develop productive pedagogical strategies for working with the diverse range of students we meet in our classrooms? As suggested earlier in my discussion of Jurecic's work with Gregory, markers of difference move the emphasis away from knowing Gregory and identifying traits of "autistic students" and toward ways that Gregory and Jurecic position themselves and each other as they navigate unfamiliar interactions. When Jurecic perceives Gregory's "difference" and sets Gregory apart from herself and the other students in the class, she needs a way of giving meaning to that difference. For Jurecic the answer entails better understanding—that is, "knowing"—the category of autism by embracing neuroscientific research. I want to suggest another way. While markers of difference come from a different direction, they nevertheless remain inseparable from broad representations of identity. Both markers of difference and identity categories contribute to an always-developing theory of the world and of people's places in it. Where markers of difference complement broader identifications is in their very singular focus on the once-occurrent moments in which people learn with one another.

No two people, as Bakhtin puts it, occupy the same vantage point in the world, so they cannot coincide; such a coincidence would result in people losing their "unique place in once-occurrent Being" (*Toward* 15). Therefore, markers of difference inevitably emerge any time noncoincident individuals interact. However, what is not inevitable is attention to and *engagement with* those markers. As Linda Flower reminds us, "an active engagement with difference" (10) is not as easily imagined or facilitated as we might hope, and Jurecic's complex negotiations with Gregory further underscore this observation. I turn here to suggest how teachers might conceptualize answerable engagement with markers of difference, and in Chapters 3 and 4, I illustrate these concepts through analyses of students' interaction and discourse in a first-year writing classroom.

Answerable engagement with difference describes a kind of attention to and way of being with others in which interlocutors seek to understand ways that they are different from (and not merely similar to) others. Bakhtin's emphasis on *outsideness* and *being-without-alibi* provide groundwork for understanding this kind of engagement. Research within composition studies has begun to move beyond a focus on dialogism to embrace Bakhtin's concept of answerability (Bialostosky; Halasek; Hicks; Juzwik, "Towards"). Following these scholars, I understand answerable engagement as situating dialogic practice within a nexus of morally weighty, responsible, and responsive ties to other humans, all centered on a commitment to articulating difference. While dialogism is concerned with what folklorist Richard Bauman describes as "the orientation of the now-said to the already-said and the to-be-said" (5), answerable engagement incorporates what Juzwik ("Towards") calls the morally weighty moment of being in everyday interaction. Answerability provides a way to do this by placing the onus on individuals to make *answerable* responses to Others and to exist without alibi. Individuals must own and acknowledge their once-occurrentness: they must live without alibi—without disappearing into a morass of abstracted "others." For Bakhtin the only *real*, actual Being is found in once-occurrent events: general categories (such as autistic students or deaf academics or glasses-wearers from Cleveland) do not exist. It is only in the once-occurrent interaction that any such terms might take on meaning and be significant. Bakhtin writes, "Insofar as I think of my uniqueness or singularity as a moment of my being that is shared in common by *all* Being, I have already stepped outside my once-occurrent uniqueness" (*Toward* 41). Any denial of that once-occurrent uniqueness is the construction of an alibi. Put another way, because an individual in a moment is the *only* individual in that position and the only one who has or will *ever* be in that position, that individual is also the only one who can actualize a particular act. Consequently, that individual cannot hide behind an "alibi"—that is, the assumption that others can do what he or she can do, or that he or she is just one among many.

Answerable engagement moves from the realm of hypothetical possibility toward actualized reality. As Bakhtin puts it, "The performed act constitutes a going out *once and for all* from within possibility as such into *what is once-occurrent*" (*Toward* 29). In any given interaction, differences emerge that impact the possibilities that are opened and closed. How one acknowledges and responds to those differences will have consequences for unfolding interactions, and these consequences require that teachers and students direct their activity toward Others in ethically responsible ways. Bakhtin's notion of *authorship* (*Art*) provides further insight into answerable engagement by framing acts as consciously chosen and performed, rather than as unconscious reactions to others' discourse. As Don Bialostosky explains, answerability deepens dialogism by incorporating the dimension of responsibility: "To think of the act as authored, not just responsively performed, as Bakhtin does when he speaks of the 'actual act/deed and its author' is to evoke the metaphor of the act not just as utterance but as written work signed for and owned up to by an author" (16). The goal, then, in *authoring* responses is both to actualize and to claim responsibility. As a kind of responsive/responsible attention to an Other, authorship necessarily involves the recognition and uptake of difference.

Markers of difference focus attention on the authored, answerable act by asking teachers and students to identify how they are naming, conveying, describing, and articulating difference in everyday interaction. Choosing to display particular markers is an answerable act; it is a response to an Other that anticipates and invites further responses. Some markers are not purposefully chosen, as I am not always able to choose whether to display my deafness, my femaleness, or my Whiteness, but I still make many choices as I decide how and in what ways these features will become apparent to those I am interacting with. For instance, in becoming aware of particular stereotypes, I might avoid some kinds of clothing or self-consciously make particular language choices. Moreover, any act of marking cannot be undone: it is "inescapably, irremediably, irrevocably" final, "an all-round definitive conclusion" (Bakhtin, *Toward* 28–29). Bialostosky glosses this passage thus:

> Having declared ourselves, we cannot not have done so. Even if we try to take back what we have done or said, all we can do is retract something already done and said; we cannot not have said it. If we say something else, it will be in the context of already having said what we said in the first place. If we say what we already said again, we will be reaffirming it or repeating ourselves, never doing the same thing in saying it that we did the first time. (17)

While markers of difference reveal difference as dynamic, relational, and emergent, they retain an element of finality and completeness, too: in each singular, once-occurrent moment, choices are made, decided, and acted upon. No moment can be reperformed. Change happens over time, across many moments, as meanings thicken and solidify as well as dissipate. But the moment remains, and it is our responsibility to make the most of those moments, made all the more precious given the limited number of them we have with the individuals we encounter in our classrooms. It is to four instances of these once-occurrent moments that I turn in Chapters 3 and 4 as students in a writing class respond to one another.

3

Reading and Writing Difference in the Composition Classroom

TO UNDERSTAND HOW TEACHERS AND STUDENTS engage one another in the writing classroom, many scholars have drawn on the metaphor of the contact zone, first articulated by Mary Louise Pratt. In classroom contact zones, students and teachers wrestle with selves, ideas, and worldviews during interactions characterized by unequal power dynamics. Within the contact zone, students take up issues of difference by reading and writing about diverse texts and by coming together with others who represent varying backgrounds, belief systems, and orientations to course material. Contact zones are not always harmonious, happy environments, and people face significant risks as they participate in them, including misunderstanding, apathy, and ignorance. Despite, or perhaps because of, these risks, part of the value of a contact zone involves learning to interact with others within such settings.

Learning to interact with others is also central to claims about the importance of diversity. Thus, contact is at the heart of each of the three kinds of diversity described by social psychologist Patricia Gurin and colleagues, namely, structural, classroom, and interactional diversity. Structural diversity, the recruitment of underrepresented students, faculty, and staff to campus, enhances opportunity for contact; classroom diversity puts students into contact with information about different cultures and worldviews; and interactional diversity highlights the everyday exchanges that occur throughout the university. Contact zone theory echoes this emphasis on various kinds of interaction: as students read, talk, and write with others, the theory goes, students realize their own situatedness in a multicultural world. This situatedness is not always easy to recognize, however. A key challenge teachers face in designing classrooms as contact zones involves motivating students to, as Pratt puts it, "clash and grapple" with divergent ideas and selves (34). In the face of opposing viewpoints, students frequently invoke a relativistic attitude: "Everybody's got an opinion," they say. "We're all different, and different is good."

When classrooms are filled with this kind of relativism, the classroom-as-contact-zone tends to feel more like the classroom-as-multicultural bazaar. In this kind of classroom, Joseph Harris writes, differences are "placed in a kind of harmless connection with a series of exotic others" (33). Treating differences as objects for scrutiny and even admiration ultimately fails to critically engage them. Such an approach, composition theorist Gary Olson explains, "deemphasizes systems of oppression and flattens out difference" (87). If everybody is different, nobody is really different. What's more, this stance contradicts the central claim of the contact zone itself—that differences are consequential for people's lives.

It is not hard to understand why students might be attracted to the classroom-as-multicultural-bazaar instead of the classroom-as-contact-zone. The multicultural bazaar renders harmless many of the risks inherent to contact zones by reducing most differences to matters of taste or preference. If classrooms-as-contact-zones are to encourage attention to what Olson calls the "crucial importance of Otherness" (87) and sponsor students' genuine involvement—not just mere presence—in a democratic, multicultural society, then those classrooms need to highlight difference and assert its significance, not simply acknowledge its existence. What I argue in this chapter is that teachers and students alike are *always* confronted with otherness and that processes of marking difference can help us recognize ways that we take up and respond to our own and others' positions. To study how people mark difference, I turn to students' classroom interaction. Writing classrooms provide frequent opportunities for interaction, from talking in small and large groups to reading and writing about texts to sharing and responding to writing. When we build these interactional opportunities into our classroom practices, we assume the value of contact with others for developing students' writing and communication skills. But precisely how these interactions help students develop a sensitivity to otherness is not well understood.

Part of the problem may be with the metaphor of contact itself. Writing scholars have critiqued Pratt's theory for describing contact in terms of physical entities violently crashing and banging into one another but offering little sense of how change happens as a result of contact. For example, Harris acknowledges the superficiality of the contact metaphor, pointing out that colliding is not the same as "intersecting with and informing each other" (33). Take the image of rubber balls colliding—when rubber balls collide, they don't change much as they bounce off of one another. The metaphor of contact remains problematic even when envisioning more malleable entities, such as lumps of clay or gaseous atoms that change form or property on contact. The fact is that students are not rubber balls, lumps of clay, or gaseous atoms, and they do not walk into classrooms carrying identities that then collide with other identities and change.

An example will help illustrate what I mean. At the same time that "deafness" and "Whiteness" are salient categories that affect how I move in various spaces, only through interactions with others do I come to understand what they mean. Put another way, deafness and Whiteness are constituted during interaction: my existing physical makeup is interpreted and reinterpreted as I and my interlocutors negotiate interactions. Thus, what is missing from descriptions of contact zones is an ability to account for rhetorical agency and the ways that people make choices as they interact with others and animate categorical identifications.

To reconcile theories of contact with the agentive, complex, and shifting nature of identity that has been forwarded in recent writing studies research, then, a different theory is needed. In this chapter, I show how marking difference can enhance the way we understand the effects of contact with others. Marking difference uncovers how individuals craft themselves in response to perceived differences that they interpret from others' bodies and interactional performances. To fill the gap limned by Harris and Olson, therefore, I show markers of difference at work in careful, detailed, and fine-grained analyses of single moments of classroom interaction, and I suggest how such markers complement processes of category identification.

While writing researchers have studied contact zones in rich and varied ways, relatively few studies have systematically examined interpersonal interaction (see, e.g., Canagarajah). More commonly, classrooms-as-contact-zones are represented through anecdotal recall (Harmon; Herrick), examination of curricular materials (Beauvais; Lewiecki-Wilson), analysis of texts produced within these classrooms (R. Miller; Murray), or some combination of these (Cole; van Slyck). Other scholarly approaches to interaction, such as sociological research on intergroup contact (e.g., Allport), have tended to focus on the effects of interaction rather than the interactions themselves. This research supplies important information about conditions that support or hinder productive intergroup contact but very little knowledge about what actually happens during those interactions (see Engberg, "Improving," for a review). So too does composition research on particular types of interaction in the writing classroom, such as peer review, neglect detailed analysis of those interactions.[1] Thus, even as scholars identify interaction as a powerful catalyst for change in students' attitudes and behaviors, they pay surprisingly little attention to how those interactions actually proceed. These interactions are important for study not despite but because of how mundane and small they are: scores of these brief encounters happen on a daily basis, and their everyday character reveals them as common occurrences in writing classrooms. The microanalyses of students marking difference in this chapter and the next address this important gap in writing research.

I analyze two very small moments of student talk in order to offer a revised approach to contact—marking difference—that explains how interactions affect students and teachers. This approach also reveals how category perceptions shift over time. These analyses identify students reading and writing difference in one writing classroom and focus on two recurring types of talk—disagreeing and telling narratives—that showcase markers of difference in action. As students mark difference, they create versions of themselves that they display for others, and because these selves emerge during interaction, all participants contribute to their emergence. For example, while I may claim the role of "teacher" when I walk into a classroom and stand in front of the chalkboard, students also participate in this construction of me as teacher by sitting and facing me, becoming quiet when I speak, and writing down things that I say. In a similar fashion, when students claim particular selves or positions, for those selves and positions to take on significance, other participants have to share in their construction. Such jostling for social and academic positions exposes power dynamics between students and teachers as they display differing degrees of control in claiming and asserting particular positions. These acts of positioning are interactionally contingent—that is to say, they depend on the unfolding interaction for their emergence and salience. They also depend on the ways that individuals interpret perceptible identity cues. After showing how students engage in processes of marking difference, I conclude by describing the implications that a theory of marking difference has for teaching writing.

WRITING CLASSROOMS AS SITES OF CONTACT: MOTIVATING ENGAGEMENT WITH DIFFERENCE

To mark difference is to recognize and respond to others' self-displays and to purposefully craft oneself within particular social contexts. This work is not always conscious. During interaction, people make minute, moment-by-moment decisions about how to act, how to accomplish desired positions, and how to respond to others. These actions are rarely carefully planned or scripted; they may even be learned or habitual (Alcoff 187–89). People are always marking difference; it is an everyday part of interactions with others. Yet marking difference is not well understood, because so many of its moves are not conscious choices. Teachers and students can nevertheless become aware of these processes and mobilize them in designing classroom environments that promote involvement with difference.

Motivating students' interactions with unfamiliar others is challenging at many colleges and universities. Study after study points to American students' increasing tendency to self-segregate into "smaller and smaller communities of sameness" (Whitt, Edison, Pascarella, Terenzini, and Nora 195; see also Astin; Levine and Cureton; Nathan). As a consequence, many schools have developed programs and initiatives aimed at encouraging intergroup interactions and promoting the three kinds of diversity identified by Gurin, Dey, Hurtado, and Gurin (see the introduction to this book). Midwestern University is no exception. One of the largest diversity initiatives at MU at the time of this study was the First-Year Experience (FYE) program, which organized living–learning communities. The design of the FYE promised students increased opportunities for social involvement, although the FYE program did not provide explicit structures for those interactions. The program's decision to leave such interactions up to students in part acknowledges the role that the three clustered classes will play in structuring formal interactions among students, but it also responds to students' general desire for control and choice in their extracurricular lives.

But such self-selection can run counter to the goals of these programs. While many factors shape students' social interactions on college campuses, several researchers, including anthropologist Rebekah Nathan, who conducted research by living as a first-year student in a dorm and attending classes, point to the increasing choice available to students as a key influence on contemporary college life. The sheer number of choices students have about what to do, where to live, who to spend time with, and what classes to take makes it unlikely that any two students' lives will converge in a significant way, and poses significant challenges to colleges and universities' ability to facilitate what Gurin and colleagues refer to as interactional diversity. If students' experiences do not often or regularly intersect with others', then it is harder to forge connections and relationships; those relationships have to be actively sought and cultivated. Therefore, to foster such interactions among students, institutions need to provide structures that heighten students' interactional opportunities, something the FYE does by center-ing students' academic and social lives on a relatively small section of campus. But even when faced with increased opportunity for contact, it is still difficult for many students to address the risks inherent in contact with difference, to choose unfamiliarity and discomfort over familiarity and comfort.

Many college classes respond to this homogenizing impulse by attempting to reduce the threat of difference by making the unfa-miliar more familiar, such as with ethnic studies courses and other forms of classroom diversity that have long been part of general education requirements. First-year writing classes also help famil-iarize students with difference by providing one of the few loca-tions, outside of random roommate assignments, where students are required to engage with others whom they have not self-selected for interaction. Like random roommate assignments, which have been studied for their impact on diversity efforts (Sidanius, Levin, van Laar, and Sears), writing classrooms demand regular, ongoing, and sustained interactions with others. Writing classrooms differ from roommate assignments in several important respects, how-ever. Roommate assignments put students together in shared living arrangements and offer extended informal opportunities for rela-tively unstructured interactions. Writing classrooms bring together varied groups of students in a more formal context and structure specific kinds of interactions among students.

Another important difference between writing classes and room-mate assignments is that while students can make choices to limit their interactions with assigned roommates, they have far less free-dom to opt out of writing classroom activities and assignments. First-year composition programs involve students in practices that insist they confront classmates and address perspectives and world-views divergent from—or even contradictory to—their own. In this vein, Midwestern's First-Year Composition program (FYC) tried to manage encounters with difference through a model syllabus that taught a simplified version of Stephen Toulmin's theory of argu-ment (see Fulkerson). This curriculum contained several aims ex-plicitly tied to students' awareness of difference: engaging multiple perspectives, taking up counterarguments, and identifying shared assumptions between arguments. The program also emphasized collaborative learning practices, most notably small-group peer review, in which students exchanged perspectives with one another. Finally, program-wide attendance and workshop policies enforced participation in these activities.

Required activities such as peer review entail a significant context in which students notice differences between themselves and their classmates. Such confrontations with difference can sometimes make it difficult for students to embrace these required activities. For instance, peer review can be vexing for students because at the same time they are told that it is a supportive and encouraging way to improve their writing,[2] the experience of doing peer review does not always feel very supportive or encouraging.[3] During peer review, students are asked to evaluate their classmates in ways that are often personally felt, to argue about ideas, and to identify possibilities for revision. These more contentious practices, even when teachers do not envision agonistic debates over student texts, can be difficult for students to reconcile with the friendly picture of peer review often painted by course instructors. As a consequence, students avoid evaluating and responding to their peers in numerous ways, ranging from providing overly general "It was good"–style feedback to engaging in social chitchat during workshops (Freedman; Kuhne and Creel; Paulson, Alexander, and Armstrong; Spear; Tobin). Because students' previous experiences with evaluation are frequently characterized by what Kevin Porter terms "a pedagogy of severity" that focuses on what is wrong with a text, students may hesitate to provide such feedback to classmates for fear it will be taken personally. Writing teachers sometimes recognize this tension and attempt to defuse it by moving peer review away from the realm of the personal, as the instructor of the FYC course I studied, Yvonne, does in her opening comments on the first day of peer review:

> I just want to remind everybody, as this is our first peer review, the idea is we're offering each other *constructive criticism* on our papers. *This isn't a judgment about the other people.* So if I say you really need to work on your thesis because I wasn't

quite sure what you were saying, it was kind of vague, *that doesn't secretly mean "'Oh my God, I hate you and I never want to speak to you again.'"* That's not what that means. It means "'Wow, the thesis was a little vague.'" *So it is not personal.* It's just *constructive criticism* that's going to *help you do better on your paper*. Okay. (emphasis added)

Yvonne's comments show that she recognizes the tension between peer review as friendly activity and peer review as potentially caustic evaluation. She says the goal of peer review is to "do better on your paper," and that to work toward that goal, classmates will give one another "constructive criticism." Yvonne's repetition of "constructive criticism" anticipates and deflects students' potential resistance to critique—resistance that is well documented in peer review literature (e.g., Freedman; Griffith; Paulson, Alexander, and Armstrong). Yvonne also acknowledges the risk inherent in criticism when she characterizes peer review as "not personal." Providing constructive criticism is not the same as making a personal attack, a point she illustrates by juxtaposing "your thesis is vague" with "I hate you." While her example is intended to be humorous through its clearly hyperbolic framing, it nevertheless urges students to distinguish comments made about their writing from comments made about themselves as writers. It further implies that when readers read texts, their responses will, or should, be about the writing and not the writer. Neither of these goals were realized by the students whose peer review talk I analyze in this book. In fact, disentangling comments about a paper from comments about the writer was one of the more difficult things students had to learn how to do in this classroom.

An example taken from a class discussion early in the semester helps illustrate the difficulty students had in distinguishing when something was personal and when they were "just getting ideas out." The conversation occurred during an activity Yvonne called "Defend Your Position." She taped the words "I Strongly Agree" and "I Strongly Disagree" to opposite walls in the classroom and held up various claims, such as "Clothes make the man" and "Everyone is beautiful." Students were to locate themselves physically around the room in relation to these claims. As the class was discussing the claim "Everyone is beautiful," Choua, standing close to the "I Strongly Agree" sign, said, "I just feel like, it's, everybody is beautiful in their own way and you know, people do know that but we just don't know it well enough to know what it is." At this, Lucy began to speak, but stopped herself, saying, "I might get in trouble for this." After some encouraging from Yvonne, Lucy finished her thought: "I feel like it's a more immature view. Not immature. Please don't take that the wrong way." This comment is an example of the kind of talk that students found difficult to distinguish: Is Lucy calling Choua immature? Or is she saying only that Choua has expressed an immature view? Is expressing an immature view the same thing as being immature? And even if they are not the same thing, is Lucy making that distinction? Lucy's worry about how her comment would come across points to the potential slippage between idea and self that occurs almost any time students talk about themselves or their writing. Indeed, students' practices of marking difference revealed again and again that not only are their own and others' utterances intensely personal, but also those utterances are inextricably tied up with their emerging classroom identities. This is one of the reasons it is so hard for students to confront difference: it has the potential to disrupt their sense of self, particularly when they encounter viewpoints or belief systems that challenge deeply held personal commitments (see, e.g., Carter; hooks; LeCourt, *Identity*; Lu; Rodriguez; Villanueva).

Every opportunity students received to interact in Yvonne's classroom gave them new material to use in displaying and interpreting markers of difference, and over time they came to identify their relationships with others in ways that enabled them to deepen their understandings of one another. Longitudinal interactions that allow people to move beyond acquaintanceship and toward friendship have been identified as important for positive intergroup relations (see, e.g., Godbee; O'Brien; Pettigrew). The FYE's design facilitates such longitudinal interaction by providing proximate living conditions and regular contact in three classes. The FYC deepens those interactions by immersing students in settings that demand attention to difference; in so doing, it also capitalizes on the familiarity students are building through participation in the FYE program.

Students' willingness to invest in classroom discussions and their ability to understand, and consequently occupy, social roles toward one another are both positively associated with the familiarity they have with one another. In one study, researchers identified friendship as a precondition for students' willingness to argue in a ninth-grade English literature discussion (Christoph and Nystrand). A more powerful illustration of the important role familiarity plays in argument is found in Lindquist's ethnographic study of everyday argument in a working-class bar. Lindquist suggests that what motivated bar patrons to argue was not their interest in reaching a better understanding or "creating the perfect syllogism" (*Place* 119). Rather, she posits that a willingness to argue had more to do with a desire to "deliver oratory" (*Place* 119). Such public oratorical performances do not aim at truth; they seek to establish and reinforce desirable social positions. To even enter into an argument, Lindquist writes, bar patrons and bartenders had to know something about who they were arguing with and needed to be able to anticipate how they were likely to be positioned during that argument. Familiarity is important to writing students, too. Their willingness to invest in potentially risky conversations and to pay close attention to what others' differences might mean for their own identities depended on how much (or little) they knew about one another. In like fashion, students' displays of markers of difference show that interactional activity in the writing classroom is often driven by social motivations rather than intellectual ones: students identify the kinds of selves they want to be, and they look for and seize on opportunities to enact those selves during classroom activity.

DISAGREEING AND TELLING STORIES: MARKING DIFFERENCE IN PEER REVIEW WORKSHOPS

Like Lindquist's working-class bar, Yvonne's classroom was rich with interactional opportunity. Class sessions were filled with students' voices in both large- and small-group discussions, and social commentary regularly peppered class conversations. With the exception of before- and after-class socializing, Yvonne structured most of these interactions, whether by leading full-class discussions or providing students with explicit small-group tasks. Peer review interactions, however, were particularly complex interactional tasks in which students responded to texts, engaged multiple audiences, and navigated different communicative styles. Ten out of the forty class meetings were given to peer review workshops. Each workshop followed a similar procedure, although with different groups each time. Groups exchanged drafts during the class period prior to the workshop, and students took essays home and wrote both marginal and end comments on the drafts. They then discussed that feedback during in-class sessions, following loose guidelines Yvonne established. Some peer review sessions stretched over two class periods, depending on the length of students' drafts.

As I explored how students identified and engaged difference in these small-group peer review sessions, I came to identify two interactional patterns in which students highlighted differences between themselves and others: disagreeing and telling stories. As seen in the transcripts discussed later, when students disagreed, they displayed markers of difference that signaled how they were positioning themselves alongside their classmates, and when students told stories, they used markers of difference to compose themselves as particular types of people acting in purposeful ways. Specific definitions of conflict and of narrative guided the identification of these types of talk in transcripts, and the analyses here focus on one example of each type of talk, taken from the same peer review session. These analyses show how students mark difference and respond to others' markers of difference in what are often very small ways.

Students' practices of marking difference were highly visible in conflict episodes, in which they made overt displays of difference, revealing some divergence in position or stance. Few of these episodes could be characterized as passionate or intense disagreements. In fact, disagreeing in any way was not a common practice in students' talk as they showed a general preference for irenic behaviors, choosing more often to affirm or agree than to disagree with or challenge others. Conflict tended to occur in debates about relatively factual topics, such as correct MLA citation and punctuation or rules of thumb for writing such as "don't start a paragraph with a question." The role students played in an interaction also affected their likelihood of disagreeing: it was rare for peer reviewers to disagree with one another about feedback provided to a writer, but writers sometimes challenged suggestions made by peers. Few conflict episodes reached satisfying resolution, whether through agreement, consensus, or compromise; in this feature, they resembled most instances of everyday argument (Schiffrin; Vuchinich). The conflict episode I analyze in this chapter reflects each of these trends: it addresses a relatively factual issue, it involves a writer resisting a specific suggestion made by a reviewer, and it does not reach a satisfying resolution. It does, however, throw the everyday rhetorical strategies of doing difference into high relief.

In contrast to the relative infrequency of conflict episodes, narratives were plentiful in students' talk. For purposes of this study, I define narratives as recapitulations of past events or accounts of projected future events that are brought to bear on the present moment. This definition represents a departure from traditional analyses of oral narratives, which have focused on a specific kind of narrative in which a single teller relates a highly tellable past event in the same sequence in which it occurred (Labov; Labov and Waletzsky). Many narratives told during everyday conversation do not look like this model. Stories may have multiple tellers, relate very mundane events, be deeply embedded in surrounding talk, discuss hypothetical or future events, or have unclear moral stances, as Elinor Ochs and Lisa Capps illustrate. Therefore, while I follow Labov's work in distinguishing narrative talk from nonnarrative talk in terms of temporality, I diverge from him in that I understand narrative temporality as not necessarily linear or straightforwardly represented in talk. Students' narratives demonstrated this nonlinear quality. They told personal stories at the beginning and the end of their workshop sessions as both entries into the workshop and transitions away from it. They also told stories during workshops about the content of their papers, about their experiences writing and revising the essays under discussion, and about their lives in and out of school. The narrative talk analyzed in this chapter shows students using their past experiences with school and writing as material for their own and others' self-constructions.

The three women whose peer review session is featured here— Blia, Lindsey, and Choua—use markers of difference to establish desirable social positions and construct identities they hope their interlocutors will find persuasive. The markers they display during the peer review interaction are influenced by what philosopher Linda Alcoff terms their "visible identities," that is, the information perceived off of each other's bodies. While Alcoff focuses on visibility, bodily perceptions are multisensory and include tactile, olfactory, and auditory means of apprehending others. By virtue of sharing physical space, the three women are noticing and taking up identifiable features and using that information as they negotiate their interaction.

I cannot say with certainty how Choua, Blia, and Lindsey oriented to one another based on perceptible or embodied cues, such as presentations of gender and race/ethnicity, classroom comportment, clothing styles and choices, age, perceived disability status, or sound of their voices unless those things are explicitly marked during their interaction. However, whether marked or not, these embodied cues do influence the identifications and representations each woman makes of the other two. For instance, they almost certainly notice that Lindsey is White and that Blia and Choua are Asian. These noticings are heavily influenced by context: at a university in the Southwest, Lindsey might be identified as "Anglo," and in the Midwestern University context, where "Southeast Asian American" is a "targeted ethnic group," interlocutors might identify Blia and Choua as "Southeast Asian American" or, more specifically, as "Hmong." Such category identifications matter to the negotiation of markers of difference because they help interlocutors make predictions regarding how markers they choose to display will be taken up by others, and they provide a sense of how salient or meaningful particular identities may be in a given context.

Thus, paying attention to markers of difference does not mean ignoring category identifications; it means acknowledging the way categories help us negotiate situations while holding those category identifications open for new interpretation and understanding. We should not—and cannot—stop using categories to identify ourselves and others, because categories are essential resources we use to make sense of ourselves in relation to others. The analyses presented here aim to show how flexibility might be cultivated in the ways we notice and talk about ourselves, our teaching, and our students.

To maintain an emphasis on the ways that students identify themselves and mark difference, the analyses performed here are fine-grained excavations of very brief episodes of talk. Such microscopic attention to talk reveals the mechanisms by which individuals display and respond to markers of difference; it also shows how students shift their self-performances within the dialogic environment of small-group peer review. Close and detailed analyses show marking difference both in terms of individuals' purposeful, active choices and in terms of minute, not-always-conscious choices that are embedded in talk and interaction. This small-scale work attends to what educational researchers Mary Juzwik and Denise Ives call "the interactional contingency" (55) of identification processes. In their analysis, Juzwik and Ives show that one teacher's identity construction within a pedagogical narrative "depends fundamentally on the responses and co-authoring of students at a micro-level" (55). Such reciprocity is central to the marking of difference. Put in terms of Blia, Choua, and Lindsey's talk during this peer review session, each woman's identity is contingent upon the unfolding interactional environment as well as the cooperation of each group member in shaping that identity. Small-scale analyses show the entanglement of identity within even the tiniest interactions and reveal contact happening on a moment-by-moment basis during singular events. In the following examples, Lindsey, Choua, and Blia try out tentative positions that are shaped and influenced by their ongoing discourse and action. In these interactions, writing and the writing group figure prominently as material for performing students' identifications and chronicling their selves.

"Comments on a Comma": Claiming the Authority to Disagree

The first example I analyze is a conflict episode between Blia and Choua about whether to add a comma to Choua's draft. In this disagreement, Blia and Choua enact a delicate dance around issues of authority and identity as they display markers of difference aimed at crafting authoritative selves. The women's talk about Choua's sentence and Blia's feedback on that sentence develops contested constructions of authority. Choua's essay, titled "Physical Beauty or Inner Beauty?" analyzes extracts from Nancy Etcoff's *Survival of the Prettiest* and Susan Bordo's *The Male Body* to argue that both texts define beauty in physical terms. The sentence in Figure 3.1 is taken from the section of Choua's essay describing Etcoff's emphasis on physical beauty. In reading Choua's sentence and Blia's marks, pay special attention to the way Blia's suggestions might change Choua's sentence. Choua has written, "Even the dictionary definition she gives is an implication of how it is a physical trait that we look for before giving the judgment to as if it is beauty or not." In the margin, Blia writes "re-phrase," while making more specific editing suggestions within the sentence. Blia's edits suggest several new versions of Choua's sentence, revisions that highlight an emphasis on fluent-sounding language rather than on Choua's meaning. To show how Blia's edits transform the meaning of Choua's sentence, consider two possible revisions of Choua's text based on the written edits. Changed elements are underlined. One revision might be: "Even in the dictionary definition, she gives us an implication of how it is a physical trait that we look for." And a second might be: "Even the dictionary definition is an implication of how it is a physical trait that we look for." The difference between the three versions of this sentence—Choua's original and the two potential revisions—is significant. Choua's original sentence references Etcoff's use of the dictionary definition of *beauty* as a physical trait. In Blia's two revisions, the first mitigates Etcoff's purposeful selection of a particular dictionary definition, and the second erases Etcoff and suggests instead that it is Choua who is using the dictionary definition to make a point about beauty. These shifts in meaning illustrate some of the risks of the contact zone: misunderstanding and misinterpretation.

The peer group talk about this sentence, reproduced here as transcript 3.1, exacerbates the misunderstanding of Choua's text reflected in Blia's written marks. At one point, Choua disagrees with Blia's suggested addition of a comma. This disagreement sets off a ten-line conflict episode that addresses not just whether a comma

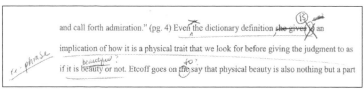

and call forth admiration." (pg. 4) Even the dictionary definition she gives is an

implication of how it is a physical trait that we look for before giving the judgment to as

if it is beauty or not. Etcoff goes on the say that physical beauty is also nothing but a part

Figure 3.1: Choua's text with Blia's written comments

should appear, but also who gets to claim authority regarding comma use. Details provided within the transcript, such as when Blia and Choua's talk overlaps as well as the volume at which particular words are spoken, provide important clues for considering where and how markers of difference emerge.[4] The episode picks up just as Blia suggests adding a comma after the word *definition,* one of the written marks on Choua's draft. Choua challenges the suggestion, saying, "<u>but</u> they don't need commas" (line 181). The four subsequent conversational turns develop this initial disagreement. Note in the transcript how Blia and Choua each uses the personal pronouns *I* and *we,* as well as how each woman builds support for her position. To help you follow the speakers' tones and emphasis, see Table 3.1 for transcript conventions.

Table 3.1: Transcript Conventions

Line breaks	What is uttered in between breaths or between pauses.
(1.3)	Number in parenthesis represents pauses measured in tenths of a second.
:	Colon indicates elongated vowel sound; use of multiple colons indicates greater elongation (e.g., no:::w).
<u>but</u>	Underlining indicates words spoken at higher volume than surrounding talk.
°well°	Words spoken at lower volume than surrounding talk.
[	Two aligned brackets indicate overlapping talk is beginning.
=	Latched discourse, continuous with previous or subsequent line.
(she said)	Transcriber uncertainty or discourse inaudible.
(*italics*)	Sounds or actions not captured in transcription.

Transcript 3.1: "Comments on a Comma"

180.	BLIA:	but in the dictionary [(???)
181.	CHOUA:	[but they don't need com-
		mas because didn't we learn over the summer
		tha::t
182.		you only put commas when you're separating
		a fragment of two sentences on either side
		(1.3)
183.	BLIA:	u::m: I've been taught differently (1.0)
184.		if you're um (0.8)
185.	CHOUA:	I was taught here::
186.		s[o::
187.	BLIA:	[oh
188.	CHOUA:	that's::
189.		but it doesn't matter:: I don't care (2.5)

Choua initiates this disagreement by turning down Blia's suggestion that she add a comma: "but they don't need commas" (line 181). In the same breath, she offsets that disagreement with the use of the personal pronoun "we," inviting Blia to share in her assessment: "because didn't we learn over the summer tha::t" (line 181). While Choua's "we" might seem to reference a shared learning experience, Blia rejects that identification, telling Choua, "I've been taught differently" (line 183). Blia's first-person singular pronoun "I" stands in contrast to Choua's use of "we" and is one of the first markers of difference exhibited here. When Blia asserts her "I," she privileges her own learning over Choua's and does not acknowledge the position of authority Choua is trying to establish. Instead, Blia displays two markers of difference—the words "I" and "differently"— to distinguish herself from Choua. These two words emphasize that the women have not shared a learning experience and make a distinction between what each woman has learned. In the next turn, Choua pushes back and offers additional information via another marker of difference: "I was taught here::" (line 185), an observation that Blia is not quick to recognize as she begins her response with "[oh" (line 187). At this point, perhaps to preempt continued disagreement, Choua ends the discussion on that topic: "it doesn't matter:: I don't care" (line 189).

Thus far Blia and Choua have used two different strategies to articulate positions of authority. Choua uses one strategy, offering reasons, when she says, "you only put commas when you're separating a fragment of two sentences on either side" (line 182). Both women use the other strategy, calling on external authority, when Blia says, "I've been taught differently," and when Choua references her past learning, "didn't we learn over the summer." Choua also names where she got her knowledge, "here::" at the university, as opposed to somewhere else. The moment Choua asserts the validity of having learned "here::" is especially significant in terms of the display of markers of difference in this interaction. With this utterance, Choua responds to two previously displayed markers: (a) Blia's verb "taught" and (b) Blia's assertion of having been taught "differently." To the first, Choua's shift from "didn't we learn" in line 181 to "I was taught" in line 185 takes up Blia's use of "I" and enables a direct comparison between having been taught here as opposed to somewhere else. To the second, Choua highlights the difference between "here" and "differently." With this marker, Choua attempts to move the discussion from one about *what* the knowledge is ("I've been taught differently") to one about *where* the knowledge has come from, moving the difference marked from authority of person (teacher vs. student) to authority of place (proximity vs. distance). In other words, Choua's claim is not just about having been taught something (which she and Blia have both experienced), but also about the heightened authority that her having-been-taught might carry in relation to Blia's. Learning *here*, at Midwestern University, has greater authority than some other, more remote learning experience. Blia does not take up this element of Choua's claim, and the topic is dropped.

Choua's withdrawal from the topic in line 189 accomplishes two things. It allows the discussion to move past this specific issue and it does so without demanding that either woman admit to being wrong. Such stalemates were not uncommon ways for students to end conflict episodes, a finding that is consistent with sociolinguistic analyses of conflict talk. "Stand-offs" are popular, according to Samuel Vuchinich, because they do not require participants to give in or to negotiate complex middle ground territory. Topic withdrawals occurred as students identified conflicting understandings of a text or, more commonly, conflicting "rules" for writing, and set those understandings against one another without seeking either consensus or shared understanding. Occasionally Yvonne was asked to mediate minor disagreements about proper MLA citation or assignment particulars. But when left to their own devices, students negotiated conflicts in performances that largely resembled the superficial contact zones Harris describes: disagreements that did not seem likely to lead to long-lasting change in perspective or orientation to a text. In the preceding transcript, for example, there is little indication that either Choua or Blia developed a new insight about comma use or changed her mind based on the other's reaction. However, this talk alone does not reveal the impact of this encounter on either woman's subsequent comma use or authority performances. What it does point to is how students mark their own and others' differences to marshal authority in the midst of disagreement using resources that have as much to do with identity as they do with writing.

The resources students draw on to make claims about themselves are often linked to their physical appearance and to the ways they are identified by others. Political scientist Nadia Brown offers an illustration of how versatile these identifications can be in describing how others' perceptions of her race/gender identity and bodily appearance—which were sometimes dramatically different—enabled her to gain access to Black female Maryland politicians. When particular features are widely identified, those features can reinforce individuals' ability to craft persuasive claims in some contexts while frustrating their ability to do so in other contexts.

Ultimately, the markers in this episode reveal how hard Blia and Choua are working to be taken seriously. As they dance around issues of authority, they also reveal that the peer review context has high stakes for them. Neither woman wants to lose face by being wrong, and instead of entangling herself further in what is already a complex social dynamic, Choua withdraws in order to find other ways of resolving the issue, perhaps by asking Yvonne after class or looking up comma use on her own. Choua's withdrawal raises a bigger question, however: how invested are students in the relationships they are forming during these peer interactions? For students to put interactional energy into a disagreement, they must care about its outcome in some way. When students display markers of difference and position themselves alongside their peers, as Blia and Choua do here, they make predictions about what positions and identifications of themselves their classmates will accept. But knowledge about how audiences will respond to various markers and category identifications is always incomplete and in flux, as when Choua's explanation of comma use is not, in fact, taken authoritatively by Blia, thus requiring Choua to display additional markers to reestablish the position of authority she wants to claim. A second excerpt from the women's talk—still about the same sentence in Choua's draft—highlights these tensions surrounding authority. Note in particular the overlaps between Choua's utterances and Blia and Lindsey's talk.

Transcript 3.2: "I'm Trying to Understand"

203.	BLIA:	I'm trying to I'm trying to understand what
204.		you're trying to say (1.5)
205.		[°(???) the dictionary definition is (???)°
206.	CHOUA:	[I think
207.	BLIA:	°shh shh°
208.	LINDSEY:	<u>are</u> you saying like that the defin-ary the dictionary definition (1.6)
209.	CHOUA:	<u>it's</u> [<u>like</u>
210.	LINDSEY:	[it's like an <u>exa:mpl:e</u> (1.1)
211.		of how: bea:uty: is a physical trait or is an implication okay wait (0.8)
212.	CHOUA:	'cause in [the
213.	LINDSEY:	[I think I know what you're trying to get at

In transcript 3.2, Lindsey and Blia simultaneously invite Choua to share what she means *and* deny her the opportunity to do so. The power dynamics emerging here are striking. In transcript 3.1, Choua offers specific details and makes particular claims about her knowledge to assert her authority. Blia, on the other hand, does not offer specifics and displays fewer personal cues. To understand this power dynamic, we must attend carefully to Blia's textual marks and the way she approximates a teacher role in her response to Choua. This teacher role, as described by composition theorist David Fuller, is one in which students' texts are flawed and problematic, and the teacher's task is to identify those flaws and correct students' writing. Consequently, because of the authority accorded to the teacher role, it is Choua rather than Blia who needs to explain and justify her decisions. The performance of a teacher audience rather than a student audience is mutually constituted in the women's peer review interaction, as when Blia says to Choua elsewhere in their conversation, "um I'm sorry I have a lot of corrections ((*laughs*))" and Choua responds with "no °that's okay°" (lines 440–41). But there are cracks in that teacher performance: Choua may accept and participate in Blia's performance of the peer-reviewer-as-teacher role, but she also pushes back at it when she understands Blia to be giving advice that contradicts what she has previously learned, as shown in transcript 3.1.

Reading classmates' writing is an area in which students come to attribute authority and knowledge of academic culture to their peers. In Figure 3.1, Blia performs an audience role that Choua may or may not have anticipated when composing her draft. The number of times Blia writes "reword" or "rephrase," X's through words, and underlines sentences that need revision suggests that Blia found Choua's writing difficult to read. As Blia responds to Choua's essay, the text acts as a site upon which Blia identifies differences between herself and Choua, most prominently differences about how well Choua writes in English and understands academic conventions. Consequently, the negotiation of Choua's sentence in this peer review session occurs at the level of word choice, punctuation, and correctness rather than at the more abstract level of ideas (e.g., what Choua is trying to say). In this workshop, then, perhaps due to Blia's reading of Choua's essay, Blia does not position Choua as an authority—or even competent—on word choice, punctuation, or grammar. Such interpretations are likely enhanced by Blia's sense of herself as a good student. Thus, despite the specificity of Choua's claims about comma use and where she has learned it, Blia remains unmoved.

It is possible that a conversation focused on the paper's argument might have generated more interactional openings for Choua. Unfortunately, the conversation that continues in transcript 3.2 shows that those openings are not recognized by either Blia or Lindsey even when Choua tries—on three occasions—to say something about what she means. That Choua makes these efforts likely indicates that she sees her meaning as a topic to which she has something to contribute. But Blia and Lindsey ignore Choua as a potential source of meaning, choosing to emphasize the text as their primary resource for accessing meaning. The opportunity to use the group conversation as a means to develop this understanding, at least in this instance, is unfortunately squandered.

These analyses reveal the claims to authority performed by Blia and Choua as interactionally contingent. This is not to say that all options are open to them, however: Choua cannot force Blia to accept the understanding of comma use she proffers, and it may be challenging, if not impossible, for Choua on her own to transform the identification of relatively unskilled writer that Lindsey and Blia attribute to her. But it is no more accurate to say that these identifications are solidified or unchangeable. As the group conversation proceeds, all of the women enact positions that shift, in sometimes miniscule ways, during their unfolding dialogue. These interactions accrete over time and inform students' willingness—or not—to participate in classroom activities, like peer review, that demand considerable attention to and involvement with others. An exchange of narratives later in the women's peer review conversation shows how dynamic interactional positions can be while continuing to underscore the challenges of holding open, rather than closing off, possibilities for identity construction.

"We Never Wrote Papers": Claiming Social Position through Narrative

Like many such conflict episodes, Blia and Choua's conversation about comma use could be likened to a game of tug-of-war as the two women pull at opposite ends of an issue. But many instances of marking difference were not so evident, nor did they all put students in direct opposition with one another. When students marked difference within narrative structures, they often did so by composing themselves as characters within their stories, characters whose representation then had bearing on the selves currently taking shape in the classroom. In the three narratives offered in this section, Lindsey and Blia tell stories about themselves as high school students; the choices they make in describing themselves have consequences for their identities in the here-and-now of the writing classroom. Through this narrative exchange, Lindsey and Blia simultaneously identify with and differentiate themselves from each other in a complex dynamic that also attributes value to those emerging identities.

When students tell narratives about themselves, they bring past selves and imagined future selves to bear on the present moment. This understanding of narrative draws on what Alexandra Georgakopoulou (*Small*, "Thinking") calls "small stories." Small stories refer to types of narrative underrepresented in analyses of oral narratives because they do not fit Labov's prototypical definition, and narrative analysts looking at small stories tend to focus on "what people *do* with their talk—and even more specifically, how they accomplish a sense of self" through narrative tellings (Bamberg, "Stories" 142). Similarly, the analyses here focus less on what Lindsey's and Blia's narratives are about and more on how they use markers of difference within those narratives to accomplish positions vis-à-vis each other.

As Blia and Lindsey tell these stories, they position themselves within the peer review interaction as certain types of people and they create themselves as characters in their story alongside other characters. These narratives occur just as Blia and Choua have finished explaining to Lindsey that she should not use the words "in conclusion" in her draft. Lindsey then tells a story about her high school experience with writing. Blia responds to Lindsey's narrative by sharing her own high school experience. In this transcript, pay close attention to the parallels between Lindsey's and Blia's narratives, as well as to the characters they introduce in their stories.

Transcript 3.3: High School Writing Experiences

Narrative 1: "We Never Like Wrote Papers in High School"

885.	LINDSEY:	<u>see</u> we never like wrote papers in high school
886.		so:: (0.5)
887.	BLIA:	oh: <u>wo:::w</u>
888.		you are <u>so:::</u> lucky
889.		[we had
890.	LINDSEY:	[no we seriously wrote
891.		I had one like
892.		my la:st
893.		my senior year I had (1.0)
894.		u:h college prep
895.		like a college prep class=
896.	BLIA:	[mm-hmm
897.	LINDSEY:	=[and we::
898.		the second semester we wrote probably two or three like
899.		two-page papers: like
900.		the first semester and then the <u>who:le</u> last semester
901.		the <u>entire</u> last semester
902.		was spent on writing a fi:ve-pa:ge <u>double</u>-spaced paper
903.	CHOUA:	huh [the who:le last semester
904.	BLIA:	[oh my
905.	LINDSEY:	the who:le last semester
906.	CHOUA:	I'm so mad at you guys *((laughs))*
907.	LINDSEY:	but anyway (???) I was like
908.		that was my college prep class
909.	BLIA:	<u>wo:::w</u>
910.		[oh my <u>Go:d</u>
911.	LINDSEY:	[so::
912.	CHOUA:	huh
913.	LINDSEY:	yeah
914.	CHOUA:	[it's so weird that
915.	BLIA:	[wo::w
916.	CHOUA:	[it's good that

Narrative 2: "We Had a Writing Across Curriculum Thing"

917.	BLIA:	[we went through <u>so:</u> much trouble too:

918.   we had a writing across curriculum thing where
            we had to write a paper for [every single class
                                        [((hits table))
919.   [five-paragraph theme
            [((hits table))
920.   °three of them° with the thesis and everything
921.   every single semester for all four years
922. LINDSEY: [cra:ppy:
923. BLIA: [and they do um: ((laughs))
924.   they do uh:
925.   u:m:
926.   they keep track of how your writing: (0.5)
927.   progresses over time (0.8)
928.   so:
929.   [that was like
930. LINDSEY: [oh:: crappy
931. BLIA: oh
932.   it was aw:ful
933.   and then we ha:d
934.   our senior science project (1.0)
935.   which is like um:
936.   a college (0.7)
937.   graduate research level sort of thing:
938.   yeah: I had to do a:
939.   exper:imen:t
940.   uh:
941.   find a:ll the research that I like
942.   you know
943.   background information I nee:d
944.   how to analyze all the experiment data that I:
945.   got off my experiment
946.   prese:nt i:t
947.   in a:
948.   uh:
949.   like
950.   uh:
951.   format like
952.   some people used overhead I used PowerPoint
953.   and
954.   it was a competition (0.7)
955.   it was so: har:d ((laughs))

956. LINDSEY: oh my <u>God</u>=
957. BLIA: [so hard

Narrative 3: "I Don't Know How I Ended Up Here"
958. LINDSEY: =[we didn't do <u>anything</u> like that I graduated
                  from a class of 36 though
959. BLIA: <u>oh:</u> I had for
960.   °well° mine was like 40
961.   40 some[thing
962. LINDSEY: [<u>yeah</u> our:s wa:s li:ke
963.   w-what was it <u>private</u>
964. BLIA: yeah it's private
965. LINDSEY: okay ours was definitely public
966. BLIA: <u>oh::</u>
967. LINDSEY: we had like
968.   kindergarten through 12 all in one bui:l:ding:
969.   like=
970. STUDENT: *((laughs))*
971. LINDSEY: =we were out in the boo:nies=
972. BLIA: [*((laughs))*
973. LINDSEY: =[never did anything:
974.   <u>ever:</u>
975.   I don't know how I ended up here
976.   no idea (1.3)
977.   but i:t's:
978.   it's worth it
979. BLIA: yeah (1.1)

The first narrative, "We Never Like Wrote Papers in High School," is Lindsey's attempt to identify a difference between herself and Choua and Blia: "<u>see</u> we never like wrote papers in high school" (line 885). What follows is a story that describes how little writing Lindsey did during her high school "college prep class" (lines 890–902). In "We Had a Writing Across Curriculum Thing," Blia relates her own high school experience, describing a "senior science project" that she compares to "a <u>college</u> graduate research level sort of thing" (lines 934–58). Hearing Blia's account, Lindsey tells a third story, "I Don't Know How I Ended Up Here," saying, "we didn't do <u>anything</u> like that I graduated from a class of 36 though" (line 958), offering the size of her school as a marker of difference. When Blia identifies with that marker, "°well° mine was like 40 / 40 some[thing," (lines 960–61), Lindsey interrupts the narrative she has been constructing in order to solicit additional information: "w-what was it <u>private</u>" (line 963). Blia confirms that it was, and Lindsey continues her narrative: "okay ours was definitely public" (line 965) and describes her school in more detail.

The women accomplish distinct positions in their talk even though their narratives follow a parallel structure. Narratives 1 and 2 display Lindsey's experience with writing "in high school" (line 885) and Blia's more specific "writing across curriculum thing" (line 918). Lindsey and Blia each use the first-person "we" to describe their past experiences, situating themselves alongside other students at their schools who performed similar actions. Both women also characterize their writing experiences in terms of habitual past actions: "we *never* like wrote" (line 885) and "we had to write a paper for [*every single class*" (line 918), suggesting that their experiences are not singular events but characteristic of the general milieu in which they were learning in high school. At this point, while the two narratives maintain a great deal of structural similarity (see Kerschbaum, "Classroom," for a more detailed analysis), they diverge in ways that significantly affect the women's self- and other-constructions. Lindsey portrays an independent internal authority, whereas Blia persistently grounds her authority in external sources.

That Lindsey and Blia build their authority in different ways is particularly evident in how they portray themselves in narratives 1 and 2. In narrative 2, for example, after Blia describes how she had to write five-paragraph themes, "°three of them° with the thesis and everything / every single semester for all four years" (lines 920–21), she adds that "they keep track of how your writing: (0.5) / progresses over time (0.8)" (lines 926–27). At this point, Blia introduces a character, "they," teachers or other authority figures at her school who evaluated student writing. In this way, Blia's chronicle is one of scaffolded writing instruction across her high school curriculum. By contrast, Lindsey makes no reference to any authority figure, teacher or otherwise, who performs any function related to the college prep class she describes. Blia and Lindsey thus establish different relationships between their narrative selves and the other characters populating those stories (Bamberg, "Positioning"): Blia acts in concert with authority figures who guide and evaluate her writing; Lindsey is cast adrift in a course that makes minimal demands on her.

These narrative selves continue to emerge as Blia and Lindsey offer more details about their high school experiences. Lindsey describes how, in her college prep class, she "wrote probably two or three like / two-page papers: like / the first semester" (lines 898–900) and then "the who:le last semester / the entire last semester / was spent on writing a fi:ve-pa:ge double-spaced paper" (lines 900–902). Blia talks about her "senior science project," which she likens to "a college (0.7) / graduate research level sort of thing" (lines 936–37). The vagueness of Lindsey's "two or three like / two-page papers: like" (lines 898–99) and "fi:ve-page double-spaced paper" (line 902) stands in sharp contrast to Blia's intensive "senior science project" (line 934). The narrative dimension of "tellability" (Ochs and Capps 33–36) is important here. Both Blia and Lindsey are situating their experiences as highly tellable extremes set against an imagined norm of high school students' writing. Adding to the tellability of these narratives are the women's accounts of their work. Lindsey uses a passive construction to describe the work she did in college prep: "the entire last semester / was spent" (lines 901–2). This passive construction alongside her repetition of and emphasis on "whole" and "entire" suggest the central focus of Lindsey's story is her lack of activity. Blia takes the opposite tack. Her story focuses on how much work she has done and the effort it involved. Blia does an experiment, finds research, analyzes data, and presents it. What's more, Blia situates herself as not only having done more work than Lindsey, but also more work than others at her school: "some people used overhead I used PowerPoint" (line 952).

Lindsey's unchallenged self and Blia's hard-working self are summarized as Blia and Lindsey finish their narratives with codas, narrative segments that signal the shift from narrative frame-space back to the interactional moment (Labov; Labov and Waletzsky).

Lindsey says, "that was my college prep class" (line 908) and Blia says, "it was <u>so:</u> har:d ((*laughs*)) . . . [so hard" (lines 955, 957). Again, the distinction is telling. Blia emphasizes her difficulty and effort while Lindsey's closing simply revisits the existence of "college prep." What these narratives show is Lindsey foregrounding her lack of activity, while Blia underscores how much activity she did. These self-constructions are reinforced by the relationships signaled to others within these narratives: Lindsey, in not naming or elaborating any other actors in her narrative, shapes an independent self, whereas Blia situates herself in the midst of performances influenced by other actors and participants. These self- and other-constructions are important to understanding how narrative 3 continues these emerging themes.

In narrative 3, Lindsey displays and solicits additional markers of difference to reinforce the self–other construction she offers in narrative 1. As Blia wraps up narrative 2, Lindsey says, "I graduated from a class of 36 though" (line 958), displaying an explicit marker: the size of her school. She offers this information perhaps as a way of accounting for the difference between her experience and Blia's. However, when Blia says, "°well° mine was like 40 / 40 some[thing" (lines 960–61), she unexpectedly identifies with the marker Lindsey has just displayed, motivating Lindsey to search for an alternative explanation: that Blia went to private school while Lindsey went to public school.

These narratives show two explicit discussions of difference, one that positions two "extreme" academic experiences and another that compares and contrasts features of the women's high schools. The markers of difference displayed center on Lindsey's and Blia's past encounters with writing in school: their academic work, their relationship to authority figures, the size of their schools, and their public or private status. But Blia and Lindsey have done more than simply notice and respond to markers of difference. The markers they display are offered up and interpreted within the context of particular racial identifications. That Blia is Southeast Asian American and that Lindsey is White means that each has different material with which to work as she crafts an identity claim.

Lindsey's desire to construct an independent self and Blia's reliance on external authority are thus not spur-of-the-moment decisions they make as they engage each other: they constitute ongoing and always-shifting cultural narratives about Whiteness and Asianness that the women draw on and revise as they interact.

In this set of narratives, then, Blia and Lindsey enact a complex dynamic of identification and differentiation that has implications for their ongoing social identities in Yvonne's classroom. To understand how Lindsey and Blia build on this dynamic to construct their identities as well as to forward a particular relationship between them, it will help to situate this narrative episode within the larger context of the women's peer review session. In other words, we might ask what motivates Lindsey to introduce the topic of high school writing in the first place. One explanation is provided in the talk immediately preceding this narrative exchange, in which Blia and Choua tell Lindsey not to use the words "in conclusion" in her draft, as seen in transcript 3.4. Note the lines in this transcript, indicated with an arrow, where Blia and Choua reference their past learning.

Transcript 3.4: "I Was Taught Also Never to Use 'in Conclusion'"

866.	BLIA:	°let's see:° (1.1)
867.		an:d (0.5)
868.		yeah and then the last sentence:
869.		I mean the last paragraph (???)
→870.		I was taught also never to use: in conclusion (0.9)
871.		°so°
872.	LINDSEY:	o:::h
873.	CHOUA:	yeah ((*laughs*))
874.	LINDSEY:	a:ll: ri:ght (1.2)
875.		do:n:'t u:se: ((*laughs*))
→876.	CHOUA:	like it's bad don't ever use that again
→877.		it sounds like they were crazy because it's all:
→878.		that's the way I used to all the time (1.1)
879.	LINDSEY:	wh-[huh
880.	BLIA:	[I don't see what's so ba:d about it

→881.   I mean don't know why I was just taught never
                         to [use it
882.   LINDSEY: [okay
883.   yeah great

Based on this transcript, one hypothesis might be that Lindsey's narrative in transcript 3.3 is responding at least in part to the frequency with which Blia and Choua each references her past instruction. In her narrative, then, Lindsey is identifying a difference between them: unlike Blia and Choua, she has not received explicit writing instruction that she can draw on in giving feedback. This explanation might also suggest that Lindsey perceives herself as somehow lacking in her preparation for writing at Midwestern University. But this interpretation does not explain the evaluations the women make during narratives 1 and 2. For example, Blia says, "oh: wo:::w / you are so::: lucky" (lines 887–88) after hearing that Lindsey did not write papers in high school, and Lindsey makes two similar evaluations when she responds to the amount of work Blia describes doing: "[cra:ppy:" (line 922) and "[oh:: crappy" (line 930). Blia and Lindsey seem to be identifying with each other over the notion that more writing is bad and less writing is good. Yet despite this shared alignment, Lindsey maintains a careful distance from Blia, a distance both cultivated through the display of markers of difference and identified through the women's embodied presence in the classroom. Indeed, as both women display parallel markers describing their experiences, Lindsey uses those markers to reinforce the divide between herself and Blia, emphasizing writing as an inner talent rather than as something learned or cultivated through practice. If writing is an inner talent and not the product of hard work and practice, then Lindsey is lucky not only because she did not have to do as much writing in high school, but also because she has an intrinsic aptitude for writing. Lindsey gestures at this identification when she says she attended a small public high school "out in the boo:nies" (line 971) but somehow still made it to MU. The markers of "small" and "public" have a multiplicative function, highlighting how talented Lindsey must have been to "end up at" Midwestern. Lindsey's narrative can thus be seen as one in which she has triumphed over adverse conditions. Blia's narrative also conveys a triumphant tone, but it is one predicated on her hard work, access to technology, and support from teachers, not innate talent.

Blia's and Lindsey's narrative tellings illuminate some of the resources students use as they identify differences between themselves and others. The kinds of stories they can tell about themselves are, in many ways, tied to their "visible identities" (Alcoff). These narrative structures make it possible for Blia and Lindsey to attribute meaning to those characteristics, to color in pictures of themselves as specific kinds of students who have arrived at Midwestern University in particular ways. Both Blia and Lindsey contribute to these identity constructions in the way their narratives complement each other and reinforce perceptions of writing as hard work or writing as a natural talent. The degree to which their visible identities complement these constructed selves is highly significant to the engagement of markers of difference. Narratives are thus important vehicles for markers of difference: they enable individuals to craft selves and position those selves against other selves being displayed in the classroom. They can also provide an irenic means for individuals to contest or challenge identity constructions because personal experience is not generally treated as material available for disagreement.

We cannot draw broad or definitive conclusions about Lindsey's, Blia's, and Choua's relationships to race and their racial identity based solely on brief excerpts from one peer review workshop, but we can learn from research on identity formation to see how these individual interactions might be similar to or different from patterns of behavior documented elsewhere. To return to Steele's work on stereotype threat, for instance, his findings about how people behave when they are concerned about living up to a negative stereotype might shed light on the relative freedom Lindsey exhibits in describing her lack of instruction versus the care with which both Blia and Choua detail what they have been taught. Blia and Choua may be aware of negative stereotypes associated with speaking English as a second language that they want to avoid in the peer review context, whereas Lindsey may not feel the threat of stereotypical evaluations from others hanging over her head. To more convincingly draw such conclusions, we need data that trace patterns of interaction over time (see, e.g., Wortham, *Learning*). Markers of difference traced through such longitudinal data can be powerful resources for unpacking individuals' identity work.

By examining how markers are used within processes of meaning-making, such as narrative and disagreement, teachers can realize their import for themselves and their students. Markers are interactionally contingent, dependent upon ongoing dialogue and the here-and-now of communication. They are not fixed cues that index identities, although they do complement processes of identity formation and category awareness. The analyses in this chapter highlight what marker-based approaches to difference and identity in the writing classroom have to offer—namely, a consideration of what individuals identify, assert, and perform as meaningful differences between themselves and others. In these brief episodes, differences in knowledge and authority emerge through talk and are shaped through unfolding interaction. In all of this, writing constitutes an important ground for students' talk. While it is not always a common ground, as Chapter 4 emphasizes, writing nevertheless provides terrain upon which students' talk is organized and understood, and where differences are marked.

MARKING THE WAY FROM HERE:
IMPLICATIONS FOR TEACHING WRITING

The presentation in this chapter of fine-grained analyses of small moments of interaction during peer review workshops reveals some of the ways that teachers and students mark difference. As we have seen, bringing acts of marking difference to the forefront of teachers' conscious practice is necessary in an educational climate in which teachers and students alike struggle to talk about difference openly and honestly (see, e.g., Hoang; Pollock, *Colormute*). Marking difference contributes to productive dialogue about difference by offering a means for teachers to scrutinize how we—and our students—respond to others in the classroom. This section, therefore, addresses the following questions: How can we identify patterns in our own and others' practices of marking difference? And how can we integrate insights gleaned from such attention into our everyday pedagogical practices?

Marking difference is one way of bringing what Krista Ratcliffe calls "that-which-cannot-be-seen, even if it cannot yet be heard" (73) into relief by helping us explicitly acknowledge what may be unconscious patterns in our everyday interactions. It enables reflection on "taken-for-granted patterns and practices—pedagogical actions so routine that they come to appear natural and unchangeable" (Juzwik, *Rhetoric* 154). I turn now to suggest some ways that markers of difference can show our classroom practices as neither "natural" nor "unchangeable," as well as provide a foundation for enriching writing pedagogy through this rhetoric of difference.

1. *Because it traces how people position themselves alongside others, attention to markers of difference can help us resist simplistic generalizations about students.* In the examples of talk analyzed in this chapter, all three women situate themselves alongside their classmates and deploy rhetorical cues to signal those positions. These acts of positioning draw on evaluations each woman makes about how others are positioning her as well as about how her own self-positioning will be received. In like fashion, as teachers we make similar moves many times over the course of a single class period as we interpret and respond to students' presence and participation. In many cases, we make these responses without knowing much (yet) about our students beyond what we perceive from their physical or virtual presence.

Reflecting on the answers to questions such as "how do I describe myself as a teacher?" and "how do I describe individual students or groups of students?" is one way to start an inquiry into patterns of marking difference. These descriptive questions help foreground what is already on our radar and put into language perceptual cues that are not always openly named in discourse. What kinds of things do we notice about our students? What kinds of things are we conscious of in our own self-presentations? Looking across these descriptions, we might also notice what is *not there*: what (kinds of) details go unremarked?[5] These are questions I have thought carefully about as I depict students in numerous situations: as I write about my teaching in professional publications, as I solicit input on difficult teaching moments, and as I tailor class activities. Such acts of description reveal what I am cueing as significant, and to whom. Listening to others' descriptions has helped me identify details that have gone unremarked in my own accounts, and reading scholarly literature on difference has heightened my attention to cues that I might otherwise have misinterpreted, glossed over, or ignored.

Explicitly describing ourselves and our students is one way of ascertaining what is most prominent in our conscious acts of identification. However, many styles of marking difference are not fully conscious but are nevertheless part of the fabric of classroom interaction and discourse. One way to probe these less perceptible identifications is by collecting stories told in the classroom or about our own teaching. Teachers' pedagogical stories have been fruitfully examined in educational research (see, e.g., Juzwik, *Rhetoric*; Juzwik and Ives; Rex, Murnen, Hobbs, and McEachen) for the ways different selves and others are characterized. In storytelling, people add texture to and make meaning from past actions as they perform particular selves in rhetorical contexts. Thus, storytelling practices show how we highlight ourselves as particular kinds of people in response to other selves in the classroom. A more specialized kind of pedagogical narrative, the "participant-example," recruits individuals present in the interactional context as characters in narratives that illustrate pedagogical concepts or scenarios (Wortham, *Acting, Narratives*). Patterns in our own participant-example narratives can reveal how we are identifying students. Also valuable are stories told about classroom events and happenings after the fact, such as those recorded in teaching journals or in dialogue with colleagues.

Some questions we might ask in examining ways that we mark difference and position ourselves and others through narrative include the following: What are the stories about? What characters populate these stories? How are those characters described and set in relation to other characters? Who is left out or not described in these stories? What are the "morals" of these stories? How are these stories situated in the interactional context in which they are told? And how are these stories connected to classroom discussions, course content, and individual or collective selves? In answering these questions about my own teaching, I have sometimes been surprised to notice some congruence between the positions identified in a participant-example and the students called on to represent those positions in the story. Making such selections unconsciously, or without forethought, runs the risk of reifying positions or identifying students in undesirable ways.

2. *Practices of marking difference can help us identify opportunities for rhetorical action and dialogue.* As we mark difference, teachers and students are immersed in rhetorical situations that both invite and foreclose discourse, that simultaneously demand and resist involvement. These patterns are visible in small ways in the preceding analyses, as, for example, when Choua is shushed by Blia and Lindsey at the same time they claim to want to know what she means (transcript 3.2) or when Lindsey backs away from Blia's acts of identification (transcript 3.3, narrative 3). To identify and capitalize on openings for rhetorical action in our classrooms, we might examine the acts of participation that are offered by and to the individuals who are present—physically or virtually. What spaces are available for teacher and student talk and interaction? What kinds of interactions happen in our classrooms, and who does, or doesn't, participate in them?

The analyses in this chapter suggest that embodied identities as well as the positions individuals cue through markers of difference impact their subsequent involvement in classroom discourse. Therefore, thinking broadly about various forms of participation and presence can move us to understand how we and our students are positioned in ways that affect our abilities to claim or assert desired identities. For example, we might ask about the moments when students experience tension between various academic and social positions in the classroom. Pursuing this line of inquiry has led me to emphasize the dual nature of the classroom as a social and an academic space. I now incorporate, from the first day of class, activities that encourage students to form social connections with one another. These efforts are not always seamless or successful—building relationships in the classroom remains a challenge—but the interrelationships between social identification and learning (Wortham, *Learning*) reveal it to be necessary work. Reflection on practices of marking difference can help us devise activities and cultivate discourse strategies that invite students' involvement in the processes of coming-to-know that are central to contemporary writing pedagogies.

3. *Considered over time, attention to markers of difference can enable us to recognize and revise how we engage with students in our classrooms.* Marking difference asks us to carefully examine single moments and to trace patterns and recurrences as relationships shift and develop. Because markers of difference are always situated in moments of interaction between multiple interlocutors, their meanings do not remain static. Considered over time—from semester to semester or even week to week—such markers can illuminate patterns and shifts in rhetorical presentation as people come to know one another in new or different ways. Revisiting individual moments from different temporal vantage points, as well as considering similar moments occurring at different times, can stimulate useful insights. For example, each semester I revisit my first day of class lesson plans. Over time, I've noticed that I record more talk about my disability in these lesson plans than I used to. That realization has led me to more openly tie my disability disclosures to the purposeful choices I make regarding how to organize classroom space and manage discussion. I have also paid close attention to stories I tell again and again, as when I describe for students my own writing processes. I now try to craft these tellings in ways that invite students' reflection on their own writing habits, rather than as stories about how they should approach writing. In this way, I make conscious revisions to my pedagogical performances based on how others have responded to my own displays of markers of difference.

As teachers and students work together in the writing classroom, they engage in processes of coming-to-know one another, and they situate themselves in various ways. Markers of difference work from the ground up to understand these processes in order to identify what differences people bring to bear on an interaction. They also facilitate reflexivity between familiar categories that are already part of our conscious identifications and the everyday interactions in which those categories take on greater complexity, resonance, and nuance. In this way, markers of difference are powerful resources that teachers and students use to engage with others and communicate across difference. Markers of difference are not all-powerful, however, a point to which the analyses in this chapter allude: Choua tries to assert herself as knowledgeable and authoritative but is not discursively recognized as such by either Blia or Lindsey; Blia claims affiliation with Lindsey even as Lindsey pushes back at those identifications. Clearly, teachers and students cannot—and do not—completely reinvent their identities through the cues they signal in their talk. Their embodied presence impacts both the markers of difference that others ascribe to them as well as the intepretations associated with those markers.

The interplay between purposeful self-presentation, unconscious choices made in the moment of interaction, and presence, whether physical or virtual, all gesture toward some of the limitations of marking difference. A second limitation is that the flexibility of identity changes over time. As people become more familiar with one another, individual identities can become less malleable, or "thicken" (Wortham, *Learning*), as they come to be understood in particular contexts as particular types of people. In the writing classroom, such understanding is heavily influenced by acts of sharing and talking about writing. It is to such work that Chapter 4 turns in examining two moments of communicative failure as students interact with one another.

4

Writing Risky Relationships: Marking the Limits of Difference

AS PERVASIVE AS DIFFERENCE IS IN EVERYDAY interaction, it is not always easily recognized, productively negotiated, or honestly addressed. Yet it is precisely through acts of marking difference that it comes alive. Chapter 3 shows how three students marked difference as they identified themselves and others in particular ways; while acts of marking difference like these are ubiquitous, they are not always successful, a point to which this chapter turns. This chapter uncovers some of the limits of marking difference by examining two moments of peer interaction when students mark difference but fail to engage those markers. To acknowledge the limitations of marking difference is not to deny its importance, however. Rather, it is to emphasize the need for practices of answerable engagement, which calls for individuals to acknowledge their responsibilities to others in communication, to maintain attentiveness to varied ways of interacting, and to cultivate openness to interactional possibility.

The two microanalyses featured in this chapter show how difficult it can be to recognize markers of difference at work. Such recognition is challenging because markers of difference are deeply embedded in ways of behaving and acting that we often take for granted and treat as natural. Recognizing markers of difference can also be painful, especially when we acknowledge the values accorded to different ways of moving in the world.[1] Tensions between these values are further complicated when writing is brought into the picture. Many students are anxious about their writing, and confronting others' writing means coming face to face with different values and expectations. Thus, writing and talk about writing are spaces where markers of difference can be especially difficult to acknowledge.

In the first episode analyzed here, two students debate a peer's feedback on a single sentence in an essay draft. The conversation that follows shows the reviewer and the writer at odds but concludes with no satisfying resolution: neither student takes up the other's perspective and they simply agree to disagree. The second episode, taken from a different workshop group, examines a set of written comments alongside the discussion of those comments. Differences that were highly marked in the written feedback were not acknowledged in the spoken talk. These two presentations of the challenges of marking difference reinforce the importance of answerable engagement—of cultivating and encouraging an interactional practice in which teachers and students are accountable to one another and willing to step forward not only to acknowledge but also to engage difference.

TIMOTHY AND EMILY:
COMPETING TEXTUAL MEANINGS

Understanding the logic behind another person's interpretation of a text can be difficult under the best of conditions simply because of how often such logics are understood to be "common sense" or natural.[2] The challenge of listening for what cannot yet be heard (Ratcliffe) in different ways of approaching texts is illustrated in a disagreement episode between two students. The conversation took place as four students—Timothy, Ian, Emily, and Lindsey (two White men and two White women)—workshopped Timothy's second essay, although only Emily and Timothy are directly involved in the disagreement analyzed here.

In his essay, Timothy has written, "If binge drinking, assault, gay bashing, and sexual abuse of women were all activities that only athletes took part in, then they wouldn't be as prevalent and problematic as they are today." In her written feedback on this sentence, depicted in Figure 4.1, Emily has twice crossed out the words "gay bashing," drawn a box around the phrase, and connected that box to a handwritten comment that reads, "I've never heard of only athletes doing this."

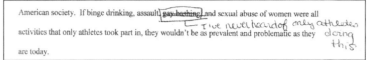

American society. If binge drinking, assault, gay bashing, and sexual abuse of women were all activities that only athletes took part in, they wouldn't be as prevalent and problematic as they are today.

I've never heard of only athletes doing this

Figure 4.1: Timothy's text with Emily's comments

Emily's comment zeroes in on a specific phrase in the list that Timothy provides, "gay bashing." The line connecting her written comment and the box around "gay bashing" suggests that by "this" she specifically, and only, refers to "gay bashing." No other part of Timothy's sentence is marked. One way to understand Emily's distinction of gay bashing from the other things Timothy lists—binge drinking, assault, and sexual abuse of women—is that she believes gay bashing has received far less media attention than the others. Thus, in challenging Timothy's description of activities often attributed to athletes, Emily may be drawing on an image of athletes that does not include gay bashing among its predominant characteristics. Unfortunately, Emily's explanation for why gay bashing does not fit is complicated by the fact that each list item, including gay bashing, is discussed in the assigned class reading (Curry). It is, of course, possible that Emily has not done the assigned reading, or that she did not pay close attention to that particular point. But what matters for this analysis is not a set of conjectures about what Emily or Timothy did or did not do or think—instead, the focus is on how Emily and Timothy discursively position themselves as they talk about this sentence and Emily's comment.

In their conversation about this sentence, both students display markers of difference that show they are interpreting Timothy's sentence in dramatically different ways. To understand the markers of difference Timothy and Emily deploy in their interaction, my analysis examines the relationship between their talk and the texts they are discussing. The emphasis here is on the ways that Emily and Timothy purposefully use their talk about this sentence to identify and signal differences between themselves. Therefore, while there are differences between them that we as observers might identify and interpret as relevant to the conflict Emily and Timothy display, more data are needed to draw strong connections between their discourse and these broader categories of difference. For example, gender (Timothy is male, Emily is female), sexual orientation (Emily is straight whereas Timothy is gay), and peer review role (writer or reviewer) all impact their approaches to each other. It is possible that Timothy feels he has particular insight into how men talk in a locker room because he is a man, or that as a gay person he is alert to circulating homophobic discourses that perhaps Emily does not notice, or that as the writer he has a stronger claim to the sentence's meaning. These factors might predispose Timothy to reject Emily's comment on his sentence. But assumptions about how Emily and Timothy understand masculinity or femininity and sexuality are, as yet, unsubstantiated by what they reveal about themselves in this conversation.

I do not study markers of difference by combing through students' discourse to test hypotheses such as those I've just described. Instead, I focus on how students position themselves during interaction and the markers of difference they use to signal those positions. Students' choices about which markers to display are influenced by their experiences, category identifications, and dispositions. But close analysis of a single episode of talk does not unearth those dispositions without other kinds of data that would enable an analyst to identify links between this talk and broader patterns. So I want to be very careful here. While I may think or perceive certain things about the students' gender and their sexual orientation, I cannot, based on a single peer review comment and a single episode of talk, definitively identify how these factors are guiding students' individual interactions. What the discussion about Emily's comment does uncover is that the two students are reading the if-then construction in Timothy's sentence in incompatible ways.

The following transcript, titled "Gay Bashing as Being Something That Only Athletes Do," is divided into four segments according to topic shifts over the course of the episode. In segment 1, Emily introduces a new topic, another piece of feedback. But before she communicates her feedback, she prefaces it by warning

Timothy, "I don't know if you're going to get mad at me for saying this" (line 1035). She then reads aloud part of the relevant sentence from Timothy's paper, effacing the end of his sentence with "blah blah blah" (line 1039). Timothy responds to her sayback of his sentence by reasserting his meaning. He and Emily start to talk over each other as the conversation builds up steam and they compete for conversational space to display their positions.

After some overlap in the students' talk, the second segment begins as Timothy interrupts the escalating dialogue to ask Emily if she has read his full sentence. At this point, the other two students in the group react: Lindsey turns to get up from the table and Ian sits even further back in his seat. Emily answers with an elongated "ye::s" (line 1057) and Timothy apologizes for sounding "really snotty" (line 1060). In the third segment, Emily reiterates her objection to Timothy's sentence: "I'm just taking it [as . . . you're saying that [someone is saying this" (lines 1065, 1067), and Timothy returns to his argument: "I'm saying that (0.5) / it i:s more than just athletes" (lines 1074–75). The final segment begins after a four-second pause. Emily says, "I still / stick to what I said" (lines 1076–77) and Timothy responds with "okay" (line 1078), ending discussion on that particular topic.

Transcript 4.1: "Gay Bashing as Being Something That Only Athletes Do"

Segment 1

1032.	EMILY:	just like little wo:rds: and repetition agai:n
1033.		but u:m (0.5)
1034.		a big thing
1035.		I don't know if you're going to get mad at me for saying this
1036.		but you say
1037.		if binge drinking assault
1038.		gay bashing and sexual abuse of women
1039.		were all activities that only: athletes took part in blah blah blah
1040.		I have nev—
1041.		like

1042.		my personal opinion
1043.		I have never heard of
1044.		gay bashing as
1045.		being something that
1046.		only athletes do (0.5)
1047.		[and that's what you say=
1048.	TIMOTHY:	[that's (???)
1049.	EMILY:	=you say
1050.		[only athletes took part in
1051.	TIMOTHY:	[no (???)
1052.		I'm saying that [if only athletes were doing this=
1053.	EMILY:	[if
1054.	TIMOTHY:	=[then there wouldn't be more
1055.	EMILY:	[but no one is saying that they <u>are</u>

Segment 2

1056.	TIMOTHY:	did you read the full <u>sentence</u>
1057.	EMILY:	ye::s
1058.	TIMOTHY:	um
1059.		I'm sorry
1060.		that sounded <u>really</u> <u>snotty</u> (0.5)
1061.		[u:m (1.0)
1062.	EMILY:	[yeah
1063.	TIMOTHY:	um::::::—

Segment 3

1064.	EMILY:	—uh
1065.		I'm just taking it [as
1066.	TIMOTHY:	[where's it
1067.	EMILY:	you're saying that [someone is saying this
1068.	TIMOTHY:	[it
1069.	EMILY:	[but
1070.	TIMOTHY:	[that
1071.		i:f
1072.		that would happen
1073.		it wouldn't be as prevalent
1074.		so I'm saying that (0.5)
1075.		it <u>i:s</u> more than just athletes (4.0)

Segment 4
1076. EMILY: I still
1077.   stick to what I said
1078. TIMOTHY: okay—

While one reaction to this conversation is to understand Emily as misreading Timothy's text, an interpretation that Timothy himself makes when he asks her if she's read his full sentence, a closer look at the markers of difference Timothy and Emily display actually reveals two incompatible interpretations of the sentence emerging through their talk. Unfortunately, each student's interpretive frame prevents Timothy and Emily from identifying the markers being displayed by the other.

Because this is a conversation about text, several lines from the transcript involve Emily and Timothy voicing written text: in lines 1037–39, Emily reads aloud the first part of Timothy's sentence; in lines 1043–46, Emily voices her written comment; and in lines 1052, 1054, and 1071–75, Timothy paraphrases his sentence. The students' conversation is guided by these written texts—the essay and the written feedback—in two central ways: the presence of Emily's written comment leads her to introduce this topic in the peer review conversation, and their different interpretations of the text generate a conflict that motivates their responses to each other. The key conflict focuses on the word "if" that starts Timothy's sentence. As Emily provides feedback, and as Timothy responds to that feedback, they display markers of difference that show different orientations to the word "if." These students' disagreement over meaning, as revealed through the grammatical structures they use to talk about the text, is highly nuanced and underscores how difficult it can be for some markers of difference to be identified.

What If?

Timothy's sentence follows an if-then logical construction: *if* the first part is true, *then* the second part is also true. But the word "if" can be read in two different ways, as Emily and Timothy demonstrate. In one sense, "if" can be a hypothetical, invoking an alternate universe in which some particular thing might happen or be the case. In this sense, Timothy's sentence imagines a world in which "binge drinking, assault, gay bashing, and sexual abuse of women" are behaviors limited to athletes. Such an act of imagination leads to the conclusion that these behaviors cannot be limited to athletes because the real world shows much higher incidence of these behaviors than would occur if only athletes did them.

Another reading of the word "if" treats the if-clause as extrapolating a current state of affairs or a claim—in other words, asking what will follow *if* this happens, *if* this is true. Emily approaches Timothy's "if" in this latter sense, treating his sentence as situated in a social milieu responding to other claims being made in the world. Her reading of his "if" attaches it to already existing claims. These claims might include the scholarly resources the class has been reading, as well as popular and local discourses about professional and collegiate athletes. Taken this way, Timothy's "if" is a response to those already available claims: *if* those claims were true, *then* things wouldn't be the way they are. So when Emily comments on Timothy's sentence, she is arguing that the if-clause is not a currently circulating claim: "I have never heard of" (line 1043); "[but no one is saying that they <u>are</u>" (line 1055); "I'm just taking it [as . . . you're saying that [someone is saying this" (lines 1065, 1067). Each of these assertions treats Timothy's claim as responding to what "someone" has said about athletes and society. Thus, Emily's critique is that this is not an already circulating claim and therefore "gay bashing" does not fit the rest of the list.

In contrast to Emily's insistence on treating his sentence as if it is part of an interplay of texts speaking to one another, Timothy understands his "if" as an act of imagination, in which he conjures up a world in which these problems in society are limited to athletes and rejects that vision because *if* it were true, *then* those behaviors "wouldn't be as prevalent" (line 1073). In other words, it is not necessary for someone else to have claimed that only athletes engage in gay bashing for Timothy's if-then construction to make sense. As a consequence, Timothy responds to Emily as if she has misunderstood his meaning, and to answer her critique, he offers two paraphrases of his sentence: "I'm saying that [<u>if</u> only athletes were doing this= . . . =[then there wouldn't be more" (lines 1052, 1054); "i:f / that would happen / it wouldn't be as prevalent / so I'm saying that (0.5) / it i:s more than just athletes" (lines 1071–75). While Timothy makes some changes as he verbally paraphrases his written sentence, he provides minimal clarification or elaboration. What results in the conversation is a power struggle between the two students over what Timothy's sentence means. Timothy's resistance to Emily's words is likely multifaceted. His reaction to the way she casts his sentence, as when she tells him, "I have never heard of / gay bashing as / being something that / only athletes do (0.5) / [and that's what you say=" (lines 1043–47), takes shape out of not only his identification as the writer of the sentence but also, perhaps, out of the way Emily provides feedback—she asserts her own experience and does not ask Timothy about his knowledge regarding what he has written.

Thus far, the analysis has suggested that Timothy and Emily perform two different readings of the "if" in Timothy's sentence, but it has not fully explored how the students display markers of difference pointing to these different readings. Crucial to the way both students' mark difference in their talk about this sentence is the verb "say," which is used ten times in this transcript. Emily utters "you say" three times as she introduces her feedback (lines 1036, 1047, 1049), and each iteration of "you say" is linked to a repetition of Timothy's text. Timothy's resistance to Emily's feedback is at least in part a response to the transformed meaning of his sentence that Emily offers through her use of "you say." Emily and Timothy's uses of "say" function to mark their different orientations to Timothy's sentence in two ways. First, their uses of "say" indicate that they are engaging in two different debates, one about meaning and one about the existence (or not) of a prior claim. Second, they employ different verb forms in pointing to the text, thus showing different stances toward the text as finished or ongoing.

What Are You Saying?

One way Emily and Timothy pattern their talk to convey their orientations to Timothy's sentence is by using the verb "say." Belonging to a category of metapragmatic verbs, or verbs employed in talking about talk (see Silverstein; Wortham, "Interactional" 172), "say" is used here to describe both Timothy's text and Timothy's (intended) meaning. In voicing Timothy's text, Emily uses the verb "say" to reference the words Timothy has written, and the verb appears ten times in transcript 4.1. The distinctions between the uses of "to say" provide a way of identifying how Emily and Timothy are marking difference in their understanding of Timothy's sentence. Their uses of "to say" are reproduced in Table 4.1, along with the spoken and textual referents of each use of "say," that is, what the "say" refers to. Note in particular the differences between examples *b, c,* and *d,* in which Emily uses "you say," and the shift in later examples away from "say" and toward BE + "saying."

The shift from "you say" in examples *b, c,* and *d* to "no one is saying" in example *f* provides the clearest indication that Emily and Timothy are having two different conversations here. To understand what this shift communicates, take a look at *e,* in which Timothy pits his interpretation of his sentence against Emily's. With "I'm saying," Timothy sets up a debate over meaning—Emily thinks he means one thing, but he actually means something else. Consequently, his goal is to move Emily toward understanding his meaning. But Emily's response to *e* is not about Timothy's meaning. Instead, she invokes an abstract "no one" who is *not* "saying" what Timothy has written (line 1055). Emily's use of "saying" in *f* does not challenge Timothy's meaning; it challenges the existence of the utterance he is invoking, as when she tells him, "I'm just taking it [as . . . you're saying that [someone is saying this" (lines 1065, 1067).

Emily's use of "saying" in *f,* then, involves a different debate. She is not focused on the meaning of Timothy's sentence, but on whether anyone has ever made such a claim. That this is the debate Emily is engaging is reinforced in *g* and *h,* when Emily suggests that her reading of Timothy's text is that he is referencing a prior utterance. Timothy does not shift his talk in response to the new debate Emily invokes, but instead returns to the conflict he has already identified between Emily's articulation and his own claims about meaning, as he reiterates in lines 1071–75 what he is "saying." These two levels of interpretation suggest one reason why this

Table 4.1: Emily and Timothy's Uses of "to Say"

Ex	Spkr	Uses of "say"	Spoken referent	Textual referent
(a)	Em	(1035) for saying	(1035) this ((anticipates forthcoming feedback))	Emily's written comment
(b)	Em	(1036) but you say	(1037) if binge drinking assault (1038) gay bashing and sexual abuse of women (1039) were all activities that <u>only:</u> athletes took part in blah blah blah	If-clause in Timothy's sentence
(c)	Em	(1047) you say=	(1047) that's **** (1044) gay bashing as (1045) being something that (1046) only athletes do (0.5)	Timothy's sentence
(d)	Em	(1049) =you say	(1050) [only athletes took part in	Timothy's sentence
(e)	Ti	(1052) I'm saying	(1052) that [<u>if</u> only athletes were doing this=	Timothy's sentence
(f)	Em	(1055) no one is saying	(1055) that they <u>are</u>	If-clause in Timothy's sentence
(g)	Em	(1067) you're saying	(1067) that [someone is saying this	Timothy's sentence
(h)	Em	(1067) [someone is saying	(1067) this	If-clause in Timothy's sentence
(i)	Ti	(1074) I'm saying	(1074) that (0.5) (1075) it <u>i:s</u> more than just athletes (4.0)	Timothy's sentence
(j)	Em	(1077) I said	(1077) what ((indirectly references Emily's previous talk))	Emily's written comment

disagreement fails to reach any kind of satisfying resolution: Timothy and Emily are having two different conversations. The shifts in Emily's use of "to say," paired with the complex interplay between spoken discourse and written text, heighten the communicative challenges the students face in figuring out each other's meaning. When Emily finalizes the exchange with "I still / stick to what I said" (lines 1076–77), she refers back to the conversation that has just unfolded but does not reassert or rephrase her point. What *is* it that she's just said?

"Say" vs. "Saying"

The uses of "to say" in Timothy's and Emily's talk hold yet another set of markers of difference showing the students' divergent interpretations of Timothy's sentence. As noted, Emily's talk about Timothy's sentence undergoes a shift in verb aspect. Verb aspect is a way of describing the duration of an activity and is distinct from verb tense, which describes the sequencing of events in time. In examples *b, c,* and *d,* Emily uses the simple present "you say," which may be interpreted as having perfective aspect, whereas Timothy shifts to the present progressive, "I'm saying," in *e.* The next four instances of the verb are also in the present progressive, which is usually said to code imperfective (progressive) aspect. Typically, imperfective aspect describes an event as ongoing or incomplete, and invites attention to the stages or components of an action. In contrast, perfective aspect portrays events or actions as fixed or completed wholes. Emily's use of the simple present thus may contrast with the present progressive in suggesting a completed, finished text, whereas Timothy's "I'm saying" highlights a more in-process view of his text. When Emily starts her feedback with "but you say" (line 1036) and then reads aloud the first half of Timothy's sentence, she is not pointing to Timothy's *meaning*, but referencing *a particular string of words* in his text. Because Emily does not linguistically distinguish between "you" as the author-of-the-text and "you" as Timothy-the-person when she moves into her use of "you say" in examples *c* and *d,* it is difficult to understand that she is continuing to point to "this claim exists in the text" rather than asserting what Timothy means or intends by his sentence. This once again invokes the slippage between text and author that is so difficult for students to negotiate during peer review.

The simple present can cast "say" either in terms of factual occurrence (those words do in fact appear in the sentence) or in relation to meaning (this is what it means). When considered in terms of factual occurrence, Emily's "you say" is accurate, but it is not accurate in terms of meaning, as Timothy attests. When he responds, he emphasizes the word "if" two times (lines 1052, 1071). Emily, interestingly, omits the "if" both times she references his text in *c* and *d:* "gay bashing as / being something that / only athletes do"; "[only athletes took part in." Removing the "if" takes the sentence out of the hypothetical realm Timothy casts it in and emphasizes instead the claim Emily sees Timothy as responding to—rather than imagining.

Emily's treatment of Timothy's text is focused on the current state of talk about athletes in society, and she uses the simple present to point to the existence of a claim within his sentence, while Timothy uses present progressive to highlight the more dynamic concept of meaning that he is focused on. This distinction in their use of verb forms can be seen throughout this episode. When Emily references Timothy's sentence in *c* and *d,* she uses the phrases "took part in" and "gay bashing as being something that only athletes do." Both of these referents describe the athletes' actions using the simple present. In contrast, Timothy in *e* uses "were doing" to characterize the athletes' behavior and stresses the "if" that begins his sentence (which, again, Emily omits in *c* and *d*). Emily's talk here asserts the present state of athletes' behavior and contrasts with Timothy's treatment of this behavior as a hypothesized habitual occurrence.

As these examples demonstrate, throughout their talk Emily and Timothy reveal dramatically different orientations to Timothy's sentence. Timothy situates his claim in a hypothetical space and constructs it as an ongoing process of meaning-making in which he describes habitual "masculine" behaviors. Emily, on the other hand, casts Timothy's text as a response to an existing claim. They do not share much in terms of the way they are approaching this sentence, except for one thing. Unfortunately, it is something that also contributes to their frustration: they both treat meaning in static terms, as Timothy argues through repetition that his meaning inheres in the syntactic ordering of his sentence, while Emily insists that meaning is constructed in relation to other texts.

Recognizing Difference Is Not Enough

This conversation is a bumpy one for Emily and Timothy: they openly recognize a difference in how each of them is approaching the conversation, and each displays several markers of difference as they try to illuminate their own perspective on the sentence. Unfortunately, they do not acknowledge the nature of that difference, nor do they ultimately act as though their disagreement matters very much. Much like Blia and Choua's comma discussion in Chapter 3, Timothy and Emily's conversation ends in a stalemate. They register their disagreement with each other but do not demand that the other take up that disagreement in any significant way. This lack of accountability points to one of the dilemmas faced by teachers implementing peer review in the classroom. Because the teacher is usually the final judge of the quality of a text, students are sometimes reluctant to rely on peers' assessments, especially if they suspect that peer feedback may challenge or contradict the teacher's. Framing peer review this way turns it into an exercise in which students temporarily stand in for the teacher, rather than one in which the students' task is to engage with one another over writing.

The win-lose dynamic of disagreement also makes it particularly treacherous terrain in the writing classroom. In this conversation, Emily and Timothy come to the brink of engaging their disagreement but hastily beat a retreat into familiar territory, behind what Jocelyn Glazier calls the borders of cultural contact. As Emily and Timothy begin to raise their voices and overlap each other toward the end of segment 1, Timothy deflects the focus of the talk away from meaning ("you say" [line 1036], "that's what you say" [line 1047]; "=you say" [line 1049]; "I'm saying" [line 1052]) toward comprehension—"did you read the full <u>sentence</u>" (line 1056). This move not only denies Emily's reading (because she has misunderstood, her meaning, her interpretation, is not valid), but it also does not acknowledge the possibility that she has something to contribute to Timothy's thinking. Timothy's shift in the conversational emphasis foregrounds the sense of misunderstanding that permeates this talk. He doesn't understand what Emily is contributing; Emily doesn't understand his sentence; and neither one of them understands the other.

The communicative malfunctions in Timothy and Emily's conversation make clear that even when differences are apparent, they are not always identifiable or easily describable. This disagreement is more than a simple misunderstanding: it involves different orientations to what texts do and how they work with other texts. Getting at these orientations requires an openness and generosity in interpretation that is not evident in Timothy and Emily's interaction. Indeed, the students' personal relationship with each other complicates their divergent stances toward and understandings of classroom texts and cultural narratives.

Chapter 3 points to how personal the act of peer review often is for students. Some teachers see these personal relationships as a barrier to productive peer review, as when Yvonne urges her students to see their peers' comments as being about the writing and not the writer (see also Spear). While it is important for students to learn to separate being told that they wrote a confusing introduction from being told that they are a confusing person, this is simply not that easy for students to do. Timothy's discussion about this episode during an interview with me underscores just how much interpersonal dynamics affected his response to Emily. Here is what he had to say after I replayed the audiotape of this episode:

> TIMOTHY: ((*laughs*)) I knew you were gonna pull this day out, I just knew once you set the tape player down, like, this is gonna come back. Um, the sentence, I think, read "if binge drinking and gay bashing were activities that only athletes participated in, the activities wouldn't be as prevalent as they are, in society." [[Stephanie: Right.]]

So I'm trying to say that if only they did it, it would be a very small number, but it's not, so it has to be a bigger group. And, I just, I couldn't get what she wasn't reading in that sentence, I just ((*pause*)) I couldn't make my mind think like her mind was to figure out how she wasn't reading it, I just [[Stephanie: Right.]] was that set off by it. And *nothing against Emily, she's a nice girl, but we just have chemistry that* ((*pause*)) *conflicts* we're—I'm constantly arguing with her, she's in my service learning group for [FYE], [[Stephanie: Mm-hmm.]] and we, *we both sort of sat down and talked, you know, we don't really get along, do we? No, no we don't, we just have that personality* (so I'm) instantly that much more snotty to her, like I was, and, yeah, I b- I just couldn't see where her mind was going with my sentence. [[Stephanie: Right.]] I thought it was pretty plain and she was going against me on it and I just couldn't see how her mind was working with it. (emphasis added)

Timothy points to his personal relationship with Emily as one explanation for the difficulty they have in this conversation: "nothing against Emily, she's a nice girl, but we just have chemistry that conflicts"; "we both sort of sat down and talked, you know, we don't really get along, do we? No, no we don't, we just have that personality."

Later in the interview, though, Timothy acknowledges his own responsibility for engaging Emily's feedback, notwithstanding whatever personality issues they might have.

TIMOTHY: There are some things, when I look over the notes, and usually it's the ones she doesn't bring up in class. It's "oh, you can look these other ones over," like "oh, these are really good notes. Oh yeah, I didn't realize I was repeating myself." She's very (good) she picks up repetition very well, must be a pattern thing, that she can just pick up and like, certain word choices that I make. Those she picks up really well (like "oh) yeah I really get that, I- I totally didn't get that—I probably should say something nice to her about that," then by the time I get to class it's completely forgotten, and then we're arguing about something again. [[Stephanie: Right, right.]] So it's- it's like, am I being as nice as I could? Am I trying to realize how she thinks as much as I can? Or am I just, you know, fed up with her and not gonna deal with it and not trying to think at all? It varies from day to day how much. One extreme to the other.

STEPHANIE: Like the amount of energy you have could kind of

TIMOTHY: Okay, did I- did I get to bed at 2 in the morning or 10 at night and what do I have to do today, do I have to go to service learning with her later? Or, do I want to be nice to her because I have to see her more today? Or do I wanna just, you know, stay in my bubble and let her be over there and let me be over here?

The string of questions Timothy asks here can be cast in terms of answerable engagement, responsibility to others in once-occurrent moments in the classroom. Such responsibility might entail interpreting—charitably—others' contributions to an interaction. Answerable engagement asks that people hold open possibilities for their interlocutors and that they engage one another as they make decisions about how to act and respond. The option to, as Timothy puts it, "stay in my bubble and let her be over there and let me be over here" is what Bakhtin refers to as hiding behind an alibi rather than putting oneself forward for engagement with another (*Toward*). In this disagreement episode, it is fairly evident that Timothy thinks Emily's got his sentence wrong. And understood a certain way, she does. But the analysis also shows that from another angle, Timothy might benefit from listening to her comments more carefully: some readers might read his sentence in the way Emily does. Is he responsible for addressing that misunderstanding? Or is that one he's willing to let lie? These are important questions as students navigate real-life peer audiences.

While understanding another way of reading his "if" might be helpful to Timothy, Emily also has an important responsibility here. Her presentation of feedback privileged her knowledge and experience ("I have never heard of" [1043]) without taking seriously the fact that Timothy has experiences of his own that inform how he wrote his sentence. Indeed, it is significant that the only item on Timothy's list that Emily chooses to highlight is "gay bashing." In this move, she asks him to erase the part of the sentence that is most visibly tied to the personal identity he displays in this classroom. As mentioned previously, why that is the single item she highlights is a matter of speculation. However, because Emily knows that Timothy is gay, she would benefit from becoming more aware of how comments like hers can function as "microinvalidations" that deny or erase the experiences of a minoritized group or identity (e.g., Sue, Capodilupo, Torino, Bucceri, Holder, Nadal, and Esquilin). In this context, when framing Emily's comment as invalidating Timothy's experience, asking Timothy to listen more carefully is problematic.

Maintaining openness to interpretive possibility is hard because personal identities are so much a part of our ways of reading and negotiating the world, and also because, as the microscopic, fine-grained analysis here illustrates, markers of difference can be deeply embedded in styles of talk and self- and other-presentation. The point is not that teachers need to perform detailed linguistic analyses of classroom talk. Rather, it is that we would all benefit from honing our skills of noticing and from adopting an ethic of answerable engagement with our students. Such practices insist on an attentiveness to the here-and-now, and they put the onus on us all to perform the best possible responses we can offer in once-occurrent moments that will never recur and that have consequences for unfolding dialogue, interaction, and learning.

CHOUA, JANE, AND MARGARET: AVOIDING DIFFERENCE

While Emily and Timothy struggle to productively negotiate the palpable difference in their discussion of Timothy's sentence, in other cases, it is not that students fail to articulate difference, but that they avoid it. This section examines a peer workshop involving three students, Choua, a Southeast Asian American woman, and Jane and Margaret, both White women. In this conversation, Jane and Margaret avoid explicit discussion of markers of difference they identify in their written response to Choua's essay. In both the recorded comments and the workshop conversation, difference remains a subtext of the women's talk that is never explicitly brought into the conversation.

The shift in this section from examining differences that are explicitly engaged toward examining differences that are avoided or elided in talk requires a different set of analytic tools from those used to parse Emily and Timothy's talk. While the analysis of Timothy and Emily's conversation entailed the use of linguistic resources for unpacking discursive choices to understand how those choices mark difference between interlocutors, different tools are needed to examine what is *not* said. To get at what is not said, this analysis examines how interactional topics are given salience and treated as either an opportunity for dialogue or to foreclose interaction.

As Chapter 3 shows, reading and responding to writing is not a simple transaction of meaning. It is also a transaction of self, in which students enact desired selves through rhetorical performances and respond to others' self-presentations. Markers of difference are integral to these interactions. But people sometimes shy away from acknowledging markers of difference because it can be painful or difficult to be accountable to—and for—those differences. For many people, similarity is less threatening than difference, a phenomenon reflected in students' impulse toward self-segregation (Astin; Levine and Cureton; Nathan; Whitt, Edison, Pascarella, Terenzini, and Nora). The turn toward similarity also pervades approaches to peer review itself. In *Sharing Writing: Peer Response Groups in English Classes*, Karen Spear writes, "For students reading each other's texts, the real value of the experience lies in the texts' potential not directly to delight or instruct, but in the opportunities they offer for revealing and shoring up interpersonal similarities. *These similarities serve to promote a safe group environment*"

(35–36, emphasis added). Sameness is here identified with safety, comfort, and familiarity. In contrast, difference, the unknown, is associated with threat and danger, especially when writers are faced with audiences they may not know well, if at all.

However, even if students in a writing classroom do not know one another well as audiences, it's important to acknowledge that all of them have past experiences—personal and academic—with different kinds of people that may lead them to anticipate misunderstanding or to resist the others in the classroom. For example, the female African American college students that sociologist Rachelle Winkle-Wagner interviews relate often feeling invisible or as if a spotlight is shining on them in class. Winkle-Wagner explains, "To be placed in a situation like this is *unchosen*—it is not only the categorical structures that cannot be avoided for the situation to exist but also the extent to which they are sedimented outside the possibilities for easy, natural critique" (90). Put another way, the classroom environment and the perceptions of others who are present impact the degree to which students feel comfortable or willing to share themselves with or receive feedback from others. The interactional dynamics between Margaret, Choua, and Jane reflect complex orientations to sameness and difference, further revealing some of the limits of marking difference. Tacit interactional styles and habits can frustrate individuals' active attention to and claiming of responsibility toward the singular moment of response.[3]

The analysis that follows takes up two sets of primary data: Jane, Margaret, and Choua's written responses to one another and their workshop conversation. The close attention to these students' comments on one another's drafts does not present these responses as representative of the type of responses students offered one another in Yvonne's class. The quality and quantity of written feedback varied dramatically from student to student and from group to group. Moreover, over the course of the semester these comments took on different shapes and forms. Therefore, the following analysis is not a representation of students' practices of responding. Instead, it highlights patterns of response occurring between particular students that provide an opportunity to examine how difference emerges through interaction with others.

Writing is an important ground upon which differences are marked and identified, and perhaps nowhere is this more apparent than in students' comments on peers' essays. Students can perceive responding to classmates' writing as more an act of criticism than an act of opening a productive dialogue about a text. When students made notations on classmates' drafts—particularly early in the semester—those notations often identified problems with the writing. For example, Jane's written comment on Choua's first sentence, represented in Figure 4.2, communicates a difference between Choua's text-as-it-is and Choua's text-as-Jane-imagines-it-could-be. Jane suggests that the sentence might be improved (or just align more with Jane's expectations for such a sentence) if Choua less baldly uses the course's vocabulary of argument to lay out the common ground between the two texts she is analyzing. Figure 4.2 also shows Choua's handwritten revision, written with a thicker pen, above the sentence.

Comments like the one represented in Figure 4.2, those that emphasized the difference between the text-as-it-is and the text-as-it-could-be, were the most common kind of response that Margaret, Choua, and Jane made in their written feedback. Some additional examples will help illustrate the range of these responses. Jane suggests to Margaret that she might say "writing" instead of "here" in the phrase "I'm not here to explain." Choua writes in the margin of Jane's essay, "I don't know what your grounding is," and Margaret tells Jane, "I think this paragraph could be two— one paragraph about the beauty industry + women and the second paragraph about beauty industry and men—you will still make the

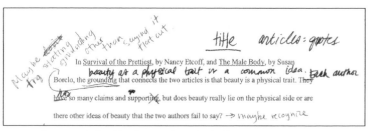

Figure 4.2: Jane's feedback on Choua's draft

same point but more organized!" In each of these examples, the students imagine a text that does something different from what they see the text in front of them doing, and they communicate that difference by describing, pointing to, or naming what a new or different text might do.

Not all of the students' written comments highlight difference. Other comments were coded as praise or as observations. Praise was more common than observation. Some examples of praise in the written feedback include Choua telling Margaret, "good example"; Margaret writing to Choua, "I think its [*sic*] good that your paper focuses on why physical characteristics are not important"; and Jane saying, "So true, I like this" next to an example in Margaret's essay. Unlike comments that pointed to difference or praised a text, observations were neutral and descriptive. One example of an observation occurred as Jane underlined a sentence in Margaret's draft and wrote in the margin, "grounding." Comments such as this conveyed the reader's interpretation of the text without necessarily pointing to change in the text. Of the forty-five comments that Choua, Jane, and Margaret recorded on one another's drafts, thirty-three pointed to a difference between the instantiated text and the imagined text, while eight offered praise and four made observations.

While coding the types of comments students made on one another's papers provides valuable information about the stance reviewers take toward the paper, also notable is the number of comments written on an individual paper.[4] Taken together, the types of comments and the volume of comments can indicate the degree to which reviewers imagine a text different from the one they are reading. Both Jane and Margaret recorded more than twice as many comments on Choua's draft than they did on each other's: Jane made nineteen marks or comments on Choua's draft and seven on Margaret's, and Margaret wrote eight marks or comments on Choua's draft and three on Jane's. Choua wrote three comments on Jane's paper and five on Margaret's. The distribution of these comments is shown in Table 4.2.

Table 4.2: Distribution of Jane's, Margaret's, and Choua's Written Marks

Reviewer	Author	Difference	Praise	Description	All Marks
Choua	Jane	3	0	0	3
Choua	Margaret	3	2	0	5
Jane	Choua	17	0	2	19
Jane	Margaret	4	1	2	7
Margaret	Jane	2	1	0	3
Margaret	Choua	4	4	0	8
	TOTAL	33	8	4	45

While the students' written comments gesture toward the degree of difference each reviewer perceived as she read the drafts, the peer review conversation about these papers is revealing not for the way students took up and talked about those differences but for the way they elided those differences. In other words, while we might expect the workshop conversation to focus heavily on Choua's paper given the proportion of comments Choua's paper received from Margaret and Jane, the opposite was true: Choua's paper received the least attention of the three papers during the women's peer review session. This is perhaps even more surprising when we observe that, as in Emily and Timothy's conversation, Jane, Margaret, and Choua's talk was heavily guided by their written comments. Each reviewer used her written feedback to structure her talk and initiate new topics for conversation. An example of this pattern is shown in transcript 4.2.

In this transcript, Jane is talking to Choua about the sentence represented in Figure 4.2. Jane orients to the new topic by reading aloud the phrase "the grounding" (line 147) and, after admitting some uncertainty about Yvonne's expectations, suggests to Choua that perhaps Yvonne does not want them to say "grounding" outright (lines 151–54). Choua responds with "I don't know" (line 155) and Jane moves on to her next comment.

Transcript 4.2 "The Grounding"

146.	JANE:	a lot of this stuff like you wrote you wrote like
147.		all right the grou:nding
148.		like you str- you straight out like flat said like the grounding is this (1.2)
149.		[and like the claims and the claims are this=
150.		[(((a loud HICCUP and banging in the background))
151.		=b-but I don't see I don't really know how she wants us exactly how to write the paper (0.8)
152.		so I don't know if she wanted us to say like oh
153.		the grounding: (1.4)
154.		and like the claim (1.9)
155.	CHOUA:	I don't know
156.	JANE:	okay
157.		I guess I don't really (1.4)
158.		and then um: (1.6)
159.		let's see (2.3)

The presentation of feedback in this episode is characteristic of the way Jane, Choua, and Margaret structured their peer review conversation. They went through each draft, revoicing the author's text and their comments, sometimes offering verbal elaboration of the written comments. It was typical in these presentations for the authors to offer minimal response beyond back-channel cues signaling their uptake (e.g., "right"; "okay"; "yeah").

As Margaret, Jane, and Choua finish reading their written comments and elaborating on them, they are somewhat at a loss regarding how to proceed. As the group wraps up discussion on the last paper, Margaret says, "is this really supposed to take the whole hour" (line 462). Jane responds, "°I don't know°" (line 463), and the group begins speculating about grades and the timeline for subsequent drafts. While the students are still talking about academic matters—although not their actual peer review drafts—Yvonne comes over and tells them, "you guys are no:t done / you are no:t done" (lines 567–68). Jane and Margaret quickly wrap up their conversation, and Choua introduces a new topic, asking the group, "do I have a thesis" (line 579). The following transcript begins with Choua's question and contains the entirety of the group's response to her: Jane and Margaret take another look at Choua's paper and point to her first sentence, saying, "=yeah, that's your thesis" (line 588).

Transcript 4.3: "Do I Have a Thesis?"

579.	CHOUA:	do I have a thesis (2.0)
580.	JANE:	oh (1.1)
581.		wait let me see yours again
582.	CHOUA:	I don't think I have one (1.8)
583.		because like I had this problem over the summer too
584.		[and they kept saying I
585.	JANE:	[well you say right here the grounding that connects the two articles is that beauty is a physical trait
586.	MARGARET:	that [yeah that is one=
587.	CHOUA:	[okay
588.	MARGARET:	=yeah that's your thesis (1.0)
589.	CHOUA:	[(???)
590.	JANE:	[did you did you find that you: found one (1.0)

In unpacking this transcript, three things are important to note. First, because the students have already exchanged feedback—that is, read aloud their written comments and elaborated on them to some degree—they no longer have a script to follow, so to speak. The written drafts, though still central to the conversation, are not structuring their talk in the same way they did earlier in the workshop. Choua, Jane, and Margaret are thus negotiating more unfamiliar interactional terrain, without the safety net of already-written text to fall back on. The second thing to note about this conversation is the way Choua invites specific feedback from her peers. Yvonne did ask writers to "set an agenda" for the peer review conversation, and she modeled examples of questions that students could use to perform such agenda-setting. But in practice, students did not take up this request during workshops, more often just asking group members what they thought or inviting reviewers to "rip the paper apart." Third, in a telling twist, rather than motivating Margaret and Jane to provide additional feedback on Choua's paper, Choua's question becomes an opening for Margaret to talk at length about Jane's lack of a thesis. This conversation begins immediately after Jane says, "<u>you</u>: found one" (line 590) and takes up seventy lines of transcript, in contrast to the twelve lines addressing Choua's question about her thesis. Granted, Jane's draft was the briefest and least developed of the three papers discussed in this workshop: Choua's draft was twice as long as Jane's and richer in detail and attention to the texts under discussion. But Jane was neither asking about nor inviting attention to her thesis—Choua was.

To understand how Choua's question turns into an opportunity for Jane and Margaret to discuss Jane's draft rather than Choua's, let's examine how the students are orienting to the differences they perceive, both in the drafts and in their interaction. As noted earlier, Margaret and Jane each made more comments on Choua's draft than on either of their own papers. Thus, they have already identified some of the ways they are interpreting each other's essays. That Jane and Margaret make more comments on Choua's draft than either of their own, paired with the fact that the majority of those comments point to difference, suggests they are noticing ways that Choua's enacted draft and their expectations for this assignment might diverge. So it is surprising that when Choua's question opens up the opportunity for Margaret and Jane to engage with her about those differences, they tell her there is no problem.

A closer examination of the markers of difference that are part of this interaction can shed some light on this issue. First, look at Choua's opening lines. She asks, "do I have a thesis?" (579) and Jane begins to revisit Choua's paper. As Jane begins reading, Choua elaborates her question: "I don't think I have one (1.8) / because like I had this problem over the summer too / [and they kept saying" (lines 582–84). In relating her summer experience, Choua explains the genesis of her question, suggesting that thesis statements are a familiar concern for her. Thus, her question is not about whether there exists a physical sentence that could be called "a thesis" in her draft, but is instead about the nature of a thesis. Incidentally, this question had been raised in several full-class discussions with Yvonne prior to this workshop, including during a practice peer review session, and numerous students voiced their own uncertainties about thesis statements in these class conversations.

Treating Choua's question as one about whether a thesis can be found in her paper provides one explanation for why Jane's draft receives considerable attention while Choua's is set aside: because Jane does not have a sentence that could be clearly identified as a thesis, it might make sense for Margaret to spend more time talking with Jane about how such a thesis might appear. Conversely, Choua's paper does not need to be discussed, because there is a clearly identifiable thesis sentence. Unfortunately, this explanation ignores the question Choua is really asking. If Choua is asking, "Can you find a thesis?" then Jane's and Margaret's answers might feel reassuring: "Oh good, you can see one." This, however, is not the spirit in which Choua has asked her question, which becomes clear when she starts to explain her summer experience and opens up space to have a conversation about thesis statements. Such a discussion is, perhaps, not one Jane and Margaret are poised to have, as they both express anxiety elsewhere in the peer review conversation about whether they fully understand Yvonne's expectations (see, e.g., transcript 4.2). Paradoxically, it is the same language that Jane critiques in her written feedback that leads her to point to that sentence as Choua's "thesis."

While Jane and Margaret probably feel uncertainty about what counts as a thesis, they nevertheless do have some ideas about what a thesis should look like. They do not, however, articulate those ideas in the peer review conversation, despite cues from Choua that she does not share their understanding of "thesis." Margaret and Jane ignore this lack of shared understanding, and Choua does not press the issue. Margaret and Jane's willingness to elide discussion of Choua's questions suggests the difficulty they have in talking about Choua's draft. It also points to Margaret and Jane's unwillingness to engage potentially thorny issues of difference, such as the fact that Choua speaks English as a second language. In addition, Jane's and Margaret's written comments reflect two orientations to difference: Jane focuses on differences as problems to be fixed, whereas Margaret performs a kind of celebration of difference.

In both her written comment and the verbal discussion of that comment (Figure 4.2 and transcript 4.2, respectively), Jane emphasizes the word "grounding," suggesting that Choua might want to more indirectly communicate that concept. In making this suggestion, Jane draws on tacit assumptions about how to use course vocabulary in formal writing. In her verbal explication, she does not explain why she thinks Choua might not want to say "the grounding" or "the claims" (lines 148–49). Instead, she implies that her feedback may be idiosyncratic and leaves open space for disagreement. In this move, Jane avoids taking full responsibility for her suggestion: "I don't really know how she wants us exactly how to write the paper (0.8)" (line 151). But just raising the question shows that Jane already does have an idea that Yvonne might prefer students not to "say like oh / the grounding:" (lines 152–53). So in her written marks and verbal discussion, Jane conveys an implicit sense that how one ought to write about grounding is different from what Choua has done in her draft, even though she does not elaborate or explain this understanding.

While Jane points out what she would not have done in writing that sentence, Margaret's response acknowledges difference in a more positive light. Margaret did not write anything next to this sentence in Choua's draft, but Figure 4.3 shows three items in her bullet-pointed list of end comments that discuss Choua's identification of grounding. Here, Margaret praises Choua for identifying the same cultural assumption she herself focused on in her paper (note that she avoids the technical term "grounding" in favor of the more informal phrase "cultural assumption") and for identifying "different ideas and takes on the situation." So Margaret points to difference, noting that she and Choua have both addressed the texts' emphasis on physical beauty but made that argument in different ways. The difference here is between two instantiated texts—Margaret's and Choua's—rather than between an imagined or ideal text and the instantiated text. But while Jane's feedback vaguely points Choua in the direction of realizing an ideal(ized) text (presumably one in which Choua does not outright say "the grounding"), Margaret's comments do not offer guidance for next steps. Instead,

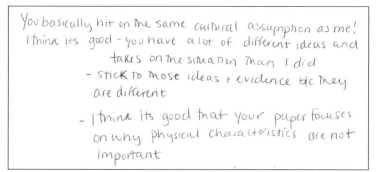

You basically hit on the same cultural assumption as me!
I think its good - you have a lot of different ideas and
takes on the situation than I did
 - stick to those ideas + evidence bc they
 are different

 - I think its good that your paper focuses
 on why physical characteristics are not
 important

Figure 4.3: Margaret's end comments on Choua's draft

Margaret's comments feed into a celebration of difference not un-like Harris's multicultural bazaar, where contact with difference in the classroom is celebrated but not engaged in any significant way.

The conversation represented in "Do I Have a Thesis?" high-lights just how much students' engagement with difference in the writing classroom is predicated more on the model of the mul-ticultural bazaar than on the contact zone. When Choua asks a question, her peers address it only superficially. The markers of dif-ference that Jane and Margaret display in their responses to Choua suggest two explanations for why they do not address the question Choua is asking. On the one hand, Margaret's approach to praising Choua for being different prevents her from critically engaging that difference or examining it more deeply. On the other hand, Jane's sense of why Choua's sentence is problematic may be intuitive and not readily available for explanation. Jane may feel she has exhaust-ed her ability to explain why she would not say "the grounding" outright. A complicating factor is that the students' talk about their papers depends heavily on the script provided them by their writ-ten comments. Unfortunately, this does not explain why or how Margaret and Jane manage to discuss Jane's draft at length, with no script to follow. In fact, none of Margaret's comments on Jane's pa-per addressed Jane's thesis or lack thereof, and the two women still manage to have a useful discussion about what Jane might focus on when she does write a thesis.

The argument I am forwarding here is that Margaret and Jane identify with each other and pick up on cues that signal to them their similarity. As a consequence, they feel more comfortable providing feedback to each other than they do to Choua. When the analyses of transcripts 4.2 and 4.3 are put in conversation with broader data, patterns in interactional styles and self-presentation might enable connections between the talk Choua, Margaret, and Jane evidence here and attention to how broader categories of race, ethnicity, and monolingualism or bilingualism are performed in writing classrooms and in writing groups.

Working from the ground up, beginning with students' talk itself, enriches our understanding of how students negotiate difference. This does not, of course, mean ignoring identity categories. Race, ethnicity, gender, and speaking English mono- or bilingually are all identities that matter to these students. For example, during a conference in which Choua and I worked together on a draft of her essay, she explained that before enrolling at MU, she had participated in a summer enrichment program for students of color. Thus, when Choua references her summer learning, she invokes experiences she has had because of her racial identity. I don't know how much Jane and Margaret knew about this program or if they even knew about it at all; I also don't know if they did any kind of summer program themselves. But the typical orientation experience for first-year students at MU involves a two-day orientation program during which little academic learning takes place, so conversational mention of "summer learning," if Jane and Margaret have not participated in such a program, may cue to them some specific ways that Choua's experience at MU is different from theirs. Set alongside discourses of diversity at Midwestern that portray students of color as needing to belong and White students as already belonging (see Chapter 1), Choua's reference to such a program might further underscore the ways in which Jane and Margaret see themselves as different from her.

Based on only one peer workshop, such hypotheses cannot be substantiated without broader interactional data. More research is needed to test and deepen these findings. The point here is to acknowledge ways that unique moments of interaction are always participating in and affected by cultural knowledge that helps people organize interaction and make differences relevant. Analysts examining such scenes usefully draw on their own identities and cultural knowledge as interpretive resources. For example, linguists Elizabeth Stokoe and Janet Smithson use the example of gender to show that just because a particular category identity is not directly invoked does not mean that the talk is not organized by tacit cultural beliefs related to those categories. Thus, Choua, Jane, and Margaret's interaction is most certainly influenced by beliefs and assumptions about race, ethnicity, gender, and speaking English mono- or bilingually. Close attention to their interaction reveals how they orient to one another, and considered over time, patterns in the markers of difference they display could productively inform understandings of how broad identity categories matter to interaction. A point of caution may be warranted here: the fact that the differences that have been parsed in this chapter are relatively small—differences in the interpretation of the word "if" or in understanding thesis statements—is not a claim that all differences are equally important. Students marshal minute differences in concert with broader identifications, not in place of them. It is no coincidence that each of the analyses featured in this book involves minority identities. These analyses highlight how difficult it can be for students to assert the selves they want others to take seriously, and they reveal some of the many forms that oppression and resistance can take in everyday interaction.

Markers of difference emphasize the dialogic and answerable relationships occurring between selves and others. In contrast to the sites of marking difference illustrated in Chapter 3, the student talk featured in this chapter gestures toward some of the serious challenges teachers face in implementing answerable engagement in their own pedagogical practice. Even if Timothy and Emily had been more generous toward each other, it's not certain they would have been able to figure out how the other was approaching the sentence. Even if Margaret and Jane had taken Choua's question about thesis statements seriously, it is not certain they would have been able to answer it satisfactorily.

These moments of communicative difficulty and failure remind us that even though answerability emphasizes the finality of individual communicative choices at particular moments, people themselves are never final. They may be once-occurrent, but they are not final. The dynamism, relationality, and emergence of difference that have been illustrated in this book reveal that teachers and students exist in continuous processes of becoming, and urge all of us to remain open to possibilities even as we make decisions about how to act that may foreclose some of those possibilities. This means making mistakes and learning from them. It also means listening to conflict, difficulty, and resistance for the sense-making behind others' acts and responses.

Coda

Returning to the Big Picture

AT THIS POINT, LET ME TAKE A STEP BACK FROM THE microscopic examination of classroom discourse to return to the institutional discourses described in Chapter 1. I now ask, "How do the circulating discourses of diversity at Midwestern University affect the way students negotiate the social environments in their classrooms?" To answer this question, we might think about how such diversity discourses invite or set up particular orientations toward people who are identified in those discourses, as when students are named in particular ways within bureaucratic procedures. These discourses contribute to an imagined version of the university in which people are constructed in very specific ways.

In an analysis of more than twenty diversity policies at land-grant institutions across the United States, higher education researcher Susan Iverson shows three ways that minority students are framed in these policies as outsiders. First, they are shown to be outsiders to the institution through arguments that they need to be better represented, more visible, or included. Second, minority students at the university are framed as outsiders within their minority group because they are exceptional or unique among their group. Third, these students are characterized as different from other groups—such as Asian Americans—who have already achieved a kind of insider status at the university. My own analysis of the MUDA reinforces the patterns Iverson identifies: members of the "four targeted ethnic groups" need to be recruited and better represented among the student body; MU needs to carefully identify and "target," from an early age, those who are most likely to succeed at the university; and groups who are "included" do not need the kind of support offered to "targeted" groups (see Chapter 1).

A more concrete example of this kind of orienting work is provided by Collin Craig and Staci Perryman-Clark as they describe how Craig's appearance as an "athletic black male graduate student" (46) was interpreted in the context of an institution where athletic programs are "big business" (47). In such an environment, "black male bodies are made most visible and meaningful in the public domains of athletic performance" (47). Such representations are often at the forefront of identity negotiations, whether or not they are explicitly commented on in an interaction. I have already pointed to the ways that Choua's references to what she learned "over the summer" (see transcripts 3.1 and 4.3) might signal to her classmates ways that her experience at MU is different from theirs. How this difference is read within the context of a writing classroom at MU is affected by the diversity discourses that circulate at MU. Conversations about diversity—which are ubiquitous in American higher education—join institutional ways of naming and classifying people to reinforce an implicit understanding of "diverse" students at majority-White institutions as outsiders needing to be better integrated into campus communities. So when Choua makes clear, intentionally or not, that her summer experience has been different from those of some of her classmates, that move may reinforce their sense of her as an "outsider" to the university who needs to be incorporated into it. Patterns of discourse in which Choua works to assert her belonging contrast with those in which Lindsey portrays her own sense of belonging. Indeed, as seen in Chapter 3, Lindsey comfortably talks about her past experiences, perhaps because they do not threaten to position her as an outsider.

Within institutional frames, faculty, administrators, staff members, and students have particular ways of talking about difference that highlight and recognize some differences while downplaying and ignoring others. The encounters described in this book are not discrete, random encounters within a university writing classroom. They are moments occurring within a particular social context that must be considered when making sense of how these interactions matter to these students. At the same time, these are moments that could have happened and do happen with regularity at universities across the United States. Despite their irrevocable uniqueness and once-occurrentness—they have never happened before and will never happen in precisely the same way again—they are recognizable as particular kinds of actions, events, and experiences.

Put another way, in the same way that the diversity discourses described in Chapter 1 are, on the one hand, tied to Midwestern's specific local context and needs, they are also, on the other hand, recognizable within a larger category of "university diversity discourse" that functions in a particular way (Ahmed; Iverson). The examples and encounters I have selected and shared in this book provide a means for negotiating and interpreting the interpersonal encounters through which differences emerge and take on meaning within particular interactions. I hope through this work to highlight the ways that we look simultaneously forward and backward to make sense of the present—backward as we interpret and reinterpret past actions and events by telling stories about them and by developing theoretical frames for understanding them, and forward as we use this new theoretical knowledge to make choices about how to act in new situations and settings.

NOTES

Introduction

1. All names are pseudonyms and identifying details are altered or masked.

2. I have lightly edited interview quotations and class transcripts to ease readability, adding punctuation and removing repeated uses of "um" and "like."

3. Brewer's discussion of the ways that communities for psychiatrically disabled people linguistically construct access has important lessons for writing classrooms.

4. Charlie shared the following response with me after reading a draft of this introduction: "what becomes clearer to me 10 years of [Midwestern State] residency later is the extent to which my awareness of categorical difference in that classroom was a function of projection and identification. Why? I was an out-of-state person in that classroom, and I am from a rural small town in [the East], even though it is also a university town. So there had to be that prior autobiographical factor in my awareness of particular differences. I should also say that I recall in composition studies training at [MU] we frequently talked about how there was more 'diversity' than might 'meet the eye' at [MU], and the 'small rural student' versus the 'metropolitan out-of-state student' was a paradigm case often cited, presuming both might appear middle class and white."

5. A move that is strikingly similar to the "proliferating categories" strategy performed by De and Gregory except that it is a way of using new sources of information within a category, not in addition to other categories.

6. Another move along these lines is to rename categories. While such renaming performs important rhetorical functions, such as a reclamation of identity by oppressed groups (see, e.g., Linton), it is sometimes done as a way of refining or redefining a category to

clarify who does and does not belong to it, a move that often has significant political import (see, e.g., Siebers, "Disability" 182n11).

7. At MU, students who leave questions blank about their racial or ethnic identity are placed in the "White/Other" category.

8. See Inkelas and Soldner's "Undergraduate Living–Learning Programs and Student Outcomes" for a description of programs similar to Midwestern's FYE.

9. Fulkerson provides a useful overview of Toulmin's model of argument as it has often been used in composition teaching.

10. I asked all students to verify that they were older than eighteen before securing consent for participation, as per Institutional Review Board guidelines; the questions asked on the demographic survey were all optional.

11. Focal students were chosen after the first workshop session. In selecting focal students, I sought to represent different classroom participation styles as well as the voices of students of color. After the first workshop, each peer review group that was audio-recorded included at least one focal student: Blia, a Southeast Asian American woman; Lindsey, a White woman; Timothy, a White man; and Kimberly, an African American woman.

Chapter 1

1. All reports and documents have been given new titles that reflect the document's role or purpose. Within quoted material, names identifying individuals, locations, or document titles are renamed within square brackets.

2. This global rhetoric also contributes to the image of diversity as a kind of "Multicultural Bazaar" (Harris) in which diversity is to be celebrated and sampled but not something that is deeply engaged and woven into the fabric of everyday life. This is the point that Hoang makes in her discussion of the conflict over the Vietnamese Student Association and the difficulties students had in talking about race and racial identities. Domestic cultural identities (e.g., being a descendant of slaves) are less marketable, less visible, and less economically valuable than are international or multilingual identities and backgrounds (see also Gal).

3. Not answering the question was also an option, although in reporting students' responses, the university counted those who did not answer the question in an all-purpose "White/Other" category.

4. It is possible that, as one reader has suggested, the use of *we* here might not be referential, but instead function as a kind of prolepsis,

in which counterarguments are anticipated before they have been put forward. The argument that the designers might be preempting, then, is that they are differentiating between an "us" and a "them"—the "us" of those who helped construct the agenda's introduction and the "them" of the general campus population. In this way, the use of *we* might be aimed at preventing that accusation rather than an effort to be inclusive or to reference any consistent population.

5. Other nouns include the word *students,* which appears ten times; *faculty* and *staff* each appears six times. Other groups referenced more than once include *people of color* (two times); *everyone* (two); and *alumni* (two). In addition, *persons* appears twice. Terms that appear only once are *people's, student body, business community, community representatives, student organizations, individuals, governance bodies, participants, citizens, community, women, committees, campus, members.*

Chapter 2

1. Within schools of education, teacher educators regularly encourage teachers to become involved in students' home communities and learn about their students' backgrounds (see, e.g., González, Moll, and Amanti; Schultz). For a variety of reasons, such moves have not been similarly encouraged among college teachers of writing, although some teachers have designed college assignments inviting students to investigate their personal backgrounds (e.g., Okawa).

2. All knowledge is incomplete in terms of an ongoing interpersonal interaction. Sometimes knowledge can be damaging and destructive, as in the problematic perception that mental illness and violence go hand in hand (see Price, Chapter 4). Other times, knowledge can be vitally important, as when teachers identify struggling students and devise effective ways of working with them.

3. For more, see Lewiecki-Wilson and Brueggemann's *Disability and the Teaching of Writing.*

4. It is important to acknowledge asymmetries in perspective between teachers and students. These different vantage points can be mutually enriching, as when my teachers' observations of how I managed in the classroom led to cooperatively designed accommodations, or when my explanations of how I experienced particular classroom situations enabled new understanding of how those activities might include or exclude me. But if teachers have impoverished or stereotypical understandings of particular identity categories and convey

these understandings to students, the results can be disastrous. In addition, teachers may identify students in ways that the students do not identify themselves (see the introduction to this book for an example). Such differences in identification can be difficult or challenging to work through, although not necessarily wrong or problematic. For example, teachers who have lived through decades of institutional racism can productively intervene in many students' experiences to recast identities of "I'm a terrible student" into a more complex and nuanced understanding of the effects of racism in their educational experiences. Sophia López recounts one such recasting in Schroeder's *Diverse by Design*. The point here is that even as writing teachers have much to bring to the table, including professional knowledge and lived experiences, we nevertheless need to maintain an openness to what more we can learn from our students.

5. For a rejection of this postmodernist approach to identity, see Moya and Hames-García and Alcoff, Hames-García, Mohanty, and Moya.

6. While I may have a broader repertoire of ideas regarding how to ensure that classroom spaces are accessible to deaf students, I don't presume to know better than they do their own preferences and needs. Indeed, perhaps because I spend most of my time in spaces where being deaf is not widely recognized as an asset or as something to be celebrated or identified as productive difference, the deaf and hard-of-hearing students that I have met have tended to avoid calling attention to their deafness or to differences in the way they negotiate social spaces. As a consequence, "deafness" is generally not openly discussed. This lack of openness is something I am working to change in my own professional life.

7. See DeFina and West and Fenstermaker for insightful analyses of how individuals use categories in talk to name identities and constitute them interactionally.

8. See Pham and Ono for a discussion of T-shirts as part of rhetorical self-presentations.

9. Social scientists have documented ways that individuals' stress and anxiety are heightened in situations where their self-perceptions do not align with others' assessments of them, as, for example, when American Indian students find themselves being identified by fellow students as White (Campbell and Troyer) or when Asian American students are asked where they are "really" from (Cheryan and Monin).

Chapter 3

1. Haswell notes that empirical research on peer review in writing studies has slowed to a trickle since the mid-1980s. Indeed, while there are recent empirical studies of peer review, they tend to elide group interaction entirely: two studies examine a computer program enabling reciprocal peer review (Cho and Schunn; Cho, Schunn, and Charney), another tracks students' eye movements as they respond to a simulated peer review activity (Paulson, Alexander, and Armstrong), and several others compare peer feedback with instructor feedback (Patchan, Charney, and Schunn; Patchan, Schunn, and Clark; Cho and MacArthur). A lone study that highlights interaction employs a pre-post-test design to assess students' perceptions of interpersonal variables and their effects on learning (van Gennip, Segers, and Tillema). Much of the writing research that does closely examine peer review talk in interaction (Brooke, Mirtz, and Evans; Danis; David; Frazier, "Co-Constructing," "Tellings"; Freedman; Gere and Abbott; Gere and Stevens; Greene and Smith; Griffith; Herrington and Cadman; Hewett; Nystrand, "Dialogic," "Learning"; Nystrand and Brandt; Sommers and Lawrence; Spear; Spigelman; Westbrook) was published in the 1980s and early 1990s. There is voluminous research on students' and teachers' classroom discourse (see, e.g., Cazden; Juzwik, *Rhetoric*; Mehan; Nystrand, *Opening*; Wortham, *Acting*, *Learning, Narratives*), but this research is primarily published in education, sociolinguistics, and linguistic anthropology and is not highly conversant with current writing studies research.

2. Ching's "Alternative Genealogy" of peer review provides an illuminating discussion of teachers' motivations in implementing peer review that have less to do with good pedagogy and more to do with managing workload. His essay provides insight into why peer review in so many instances ignores the ethical dilemmas students face, dilemmas that are particularly well illustrated in Griffith's powerful study, "Writing Ethics."

3. The title of Fernsten's essay, "Peer Response: Helpful Pedagogy or Hellish Event," explicitly evokes this tension.

4. Markers of difference take on a variety of forms and can emerge through word choice, emphasis, and volume, as well as other verbal cues for signaling meaning. Considered across time and contexts, the detail in this transcript is designed to enable attention to as many potential markers of difference as possible. Other valuable sources of meaning-making not transcribed here include gestures

(Godbee; Thompson; Wolfe) and gaze (Everts), both of which would contribute to interpretations of how students signal and reinforce particular interpretations and cues.

5. Goodburn discusses her own elision of race in depicting a classroom scene.

Chapter 4

1. To take a mundane example, consider some kinds of participation that are valued in the composition classroom, such as speaking regularly during class discussions, or values accorded to particular styles of dress or bodily adornment.

2. Tannen's work (*You, You're*) can be viewed as a way of making available for examination patterns in kinds of talk—e.g., between men and women or mothers and daughters—that can enable people to change problematic ways of speaking and interpreting discourse.

3. It is important to also acknowledge the ways in which silence and/or withdrawal from interaction are means of maintaining self in the face of resistance or discrimination and that responsibility extends toward the self as well as toward others.

4. In counting the marks and comments on a draft, I clustered marks aimed at a single point. For example, when Jane underlined one of Choua's sentences and wrote in the margins, "what cultural assumption," both the underline and the comment were treated as one unit for counting purposes. In some cases, the only mark was a circle around some text or the crossing out of a word or correction of a typo with no accompanying explanation, while in other cases there was written feedback that was not specifically linked to a section of the text. These marks were all counted separately. End comments were broken up according to specific points. Where possible, this followed the commenter's own separation of topics. For example, Margaret recorded her end comments on Jane's and Choua's papers as a series of bullet points. Each bullet point was counted separately rather than together as a single unit.

WORKS CITED

Ahmed, Sara. *On Being Included: Racism and Diversity in Institutional Life.* Durham: Duke UP, 2012. Print.

Alcoff, Linda Martín. *Visible Identities: Race, Gender, and the Self.* New York: Oxford UP, 2006. Print.

Alcoff, Linda Martín, Michael Hames-García, Satya P. Mohanty, and Paula M. L. Moya, eds. *Identity Politics Reconsidered.* New York: Palgrave Macmillan, 2006. Print.

Alexander, Jonathan. *Literacy, Sexuality, Pedagogy: Theory and Practice for Composition Studies.* Logan: Utah State UP, 2008. Print.

Allport, Gordon W. *The Nature of Prejudice.* 1954. Reading: Addison-Wesley, 1979. Print.

Astin, Alexander. "Diversity and Multiculturalism on the Campus: How Are Students Affected?" *Change* 25.2 (1993): 44–49. Print.

Bakhtin, Mikhail. *Art and Answerability: Early Philosophical Essays by M. M. Bakhtin.* Trans. Vadim Liapunov. Ed. Michael Holquist and Vadim Liapunov. Austin: U of Texas P, 1990. Print.

———. *Toward a Philosophy of the Act.* Trans. Vadim Liapunov. Ed. Vadim Liapunov and Michael Holquist. Austin: U of Texas P, 1993. Print.

Bamberg, Michael. "Positioning between Structure and Performance." *Journal of Narrative and Life History* 7.1-4 (1997): 335–42. Print.

———. "Stories: Big or Small? Why Do We Care?" *Narrative Inquiry* 16.1 (2006): 139–47. Web. 21 Feb. 2009.

Bauman, Richard. *A World of Others' Words: Cross Cultural Perspectives on Intertextuality.* Malden: Blackwell, 2004. Print.

Beaufort, Anne. *College Writing and Beyond: A New Framework for University Writing Instruction.* Logan: Utah State UP, 2007. Print.

Beauvais, Paul Jude. "First Contact: Composition Students' Close Encounters with College Culture." Wolff 21–47.

Bell, Joyce M., and Douglas Hartmann. "Diversity in Everyday Discourse: The Cultural Ambiguities and Consequences of 'Happy Talk.'" *American Sociological Review* 72.6 (2007): 895–914. Print.

Bialostosky, Don H. "Bakhtin's 'Rough Draft': *Toward a Philosophy of the Act*, Ethics, and Composition Studies." *Rhetoric Review* 18.1 (1999): 6–25. Print.

Blommaert, Jan, and Jef Verschueren. *Debating Diversity: Analysing the Discourse of Tolerance*. London: Routledge, 1998. Print.

Bonilla-Silva, Eduardo. *Racism without Racists: Color-Blind Racism and Racial Inequality in Contemporary America*. 3rd ed. Lanham: Rowman, 2010. Print.

Bordo, Susan. *The Male Body: A New Look at Men in Public and in Private*. New York: Farrar, 1999. Print.

Brayboy, Bryan McKinley Jones. "Hiding in the Ivy: American Indian Students and Visibility in Elite Educational Settings." *Harvard Educational Review* 74.2 (2004): 125–52. Print.

Brewer, Elizabeth. "Community." In "Multimodality in Motion: Disability and Kairotic Space." Webtext collection. By Melanie Yergeau, Elizabeth Brewer, Stephanie Kerschbaum, Sushil Oswal, Margaret Price, Michael Salvo, Cynthia Selfe, and Franny Howes. *Kairos: A Journal of Rhetoric, Technology, and Pedagogy* 18.1 (2013): n. pag. Web. 24 Sept. 2013.

Brooke, Robert, Ruth Mirtz and Rick Evans. *Small Groups in Writing Workshops: Invitations to a Writer's Life*. Urbana: NCTE, 1994. Print.

Brown, Kevin D. "Now is the Appropriate Time for Selective Higher Education Programs to Collect Racial and Ethnic Data on its Black Applicants and Students." *Thurgood Marshall Law Review* 34 (2009): 287–321. *Social Science Research Network*. Web. 12 July 2012.

Brown, Nadia E. "Negotiating the Insider/Outsider Status: Black Feminist Ethnography and Legislative Studies." *Journal of Feminist Scholarship* 3 (2012): 19–34. Print.

Brown, Stephen Gilbert, and Sidney I. Dobrin, eds. *Ethnography Unbound: From Theory Shock to Critical Praxis*. Albany: State U of New York P, 2004. Print.

Brueggemann, Brenda Jo, Linda Feldmeier White, Patricia A. Dunn, Barbara A. Heifferon, and Johnson Cheu. "Becoming Visible: Lessons in Disability." *College Composition and Communication* 52.3 (2001): 368–98. Print.

Burgess, Amy, and Roz Ivanič. "Writing and Being Written: Issues of Identity Across Timescales." *Written Communication* 27.2 (2010): 228–55. Print.

Campbell, Mary E., and Lisa Troyer. "The Implications of Racial Misclassification by Observers." *American Sociological Review* 72.5 (2007): 750–65. Print.

Canagarajah, A. Suresh. "Safe Houses in the Contact Zone: Coping Strategies of African-American Students in the Academy." *College Composition and Communication* 48.2 (1997): 173–96. Print.

Carroll, Lee Ann. *Rehearsing New Roles: How College Students Develop as Writers.* Carbondale: Southern Illinois UP, 2002. Print.

Carter, Shannon. "Living Inside the Bible (Belt)." *College English* 69.6 (2007): 572–95. Print.

Cazden, Courtney B. *Classroom Discourse: The Language of Teaching and Learning.* 2nd ed. Portsmouth: Heinemann, 2001. Print.

Chang, Mitchell J. "The Positive Educational Effects of Racial Diversity on Campus." *Diversity Challenged: Evidence on the Impact of Affirmative Action.* Ed. Gary Orfield with Michal Kurlaender. Cambridge: Harvard Educ., 2001. 175–86. Print.

Chang, Mitchell J., Nida Denson, Victor Sáenz, and Kimberly Misa. "The Educational Benefits of Sustaining Cross-Racial Interaction among Undergraduates." *Journal of Higher Education* 77.3 (2006): 430–55. Print.

Cheryan, Sapna, and Benoît Monin. "'Where are You *Really* From?': Asian Americans and Identity Denial." *Journal of Personality and Social Psychology* 89.5 (2005): 717–30. Print.

Ching, Kory Lawson. "Peer Response in the Composition Classroom: An Alternative Genealogy." *Rhetoric Review* 26.3 (2007): 303–19. Print.

Chiseri-Strater, Elizabeth. *Academic Literacies: The Public and Private Discourse of University Students.* Portsmouth, NH: Boynton/Cook, 1991. Print.

Cho, Kwangsu, and Charles MacArthur. "Student Revision with Peer and Expert Reviewing." *Learning and Instruction* 20.4 (2010): 328–38. *ScienceDirect.* Web. 7 Mar. 2012.

Cho, Kwangsu, and Christian D. Schunn. "Scaffolded Writing and Rewriting in the Discipline: A Web-Based Reciprocal Peer Review System." *Computers and Education* 48.3 (2007): 409–26. Print.

Cho, Kwangsu, Christian D. Schunn, and Davida Charney. "Commenting on Writing: Typology and Perceived Helpfulness of Comments from Novice Peer Reviewers and Subject Matter Experts." *Written Communication* 23.3 (2006): 260–94. Print.

Christoph, Julie Nelson, and Martin Nystrand. "Taking Risks, Negotiating Relationships: One Teacher's Transition toward a Dialogic Classroom." *Research in the Teaching of English* 36.2 (2001): 249–86. Print.

Cole, Daniel. "Writing Removal and Resistance: Native American Rhetoric in the Composition Classroom." *College Composition and Communication* 63.1 (2011): 122–44. Print.

Crable, Bryan. "Symbolizing Motion: Burke's Dialectic and Rhetoric of the Body." *Rhetoric Review* 22.2 (2003): 121–37. Print.

Craig, Collin Lamont, and Staci Maree Perryman-Clark. "Troubling the Boundaries: (De)Constructing WPA Identities at the Intersections of Race and Gender." *WPA: Writing Program Administration* 34.2 (2011): 37–58. Print.

Crenshaw, Kimberlé Williams. "Mapping the Margins: Intersectionality, Identity Politics, and Violence against Women of Color." *Critical Race Theory: The Key Writings that Formed the Movement.* Ed. Kimberlé Crenshaw, Neil Gotanda, Gary Peller, and Kendall Thomas. New York: New, 1995. 357–83. Print.

Curry, Timothy Jon. "Booze and Bar Fights: A Journey to the Dark Side of College Athletics." *Masculinities, Gender Relations, and Sport.* Ed. Jim McKay, Michael A. Messner, and Don Sabo. Thousand Oaks: SAGE, 2000. 162–75. Print.

Cushman, Ellen. "Toward a Rhetoric of Self-Representation: Identity Politics in Indian Country and Rhetoric and Composition." *College Composition and Communication* 60.2 (2008): 321–65. Print.

Danis, Mary Francine. "Peer Response Groups in a College Writing Workshop: Students' Suggestions for Revising Compositions." Diss. Michigan State U, 1980. Microfilm.

David, Denise. "An Ethnographic Investigation of Talk in Small Group Writing Workshops in a College Writing Class." Diss. State U of New York at Buffalo, 1986. Print.

De, Esha Niyogi, and Donna Uthus Gregory. "Decolonizing the Classroom: Freshman Composition in a Multicultural Setting." *Writing in Multicultural Settings.* Ed. Carol Severino, Juan C. Guerra, and Johnnella E. Butler. New York: MLA, 1997. 118–32. Print.

DeFina, Anna. *Identity in Narrative: A Study of Immigrant Discourse.* Philadelphia: Benjamins, 2003. Print.

Delpit, Lisa. *Other People's Children: Cultural Conflict in the Classroom.* New York: New, 1995. Print.

Dryer, Dylan B. "At a Mirror, Darkly: The Imagined Undergraduate Writers of Ten Novice Composition Instructors." *College Composition and Communication* 63.3 (2012): 420–52. Print.

Duffy, John. "Virtuous Arguments." *Inside Higher Ed* 16 Mar. 2012. Web. 16 Mar. 2012.

———. *Writing from These Roots: Literacy in a Hmong-American Community.* Honolulu: U of Hawaii P, 2007. Print.

Duffy, John, and Rebecca Dorner. "The Pathos of 'Mindblindness': Autism, Science, and Sadness in 'Theory of Mind' Narratives." *Journal of Literary and Cultural Disability Studies* 5.2 (2011): 201–16. Print.

Dunn, Patricia A. *Learning Re-Abled: The Learning Disability Controversy and Composition Studies.* Portsmouth: Boynton/Cook, 1995. *WAC Clearinghouse.* Web. 27 Mar. 2011.

Duranti, Alessandro, and Charles Goodwin, eds. *Rethinking Context: Language as an Interactive Phenomenon.* Cambridge: Cambridge UP, 1992. Print.

Dyson, Anne Haas. *Writing Superheroes: Contemporary Childhood, Popular Culture, and Classroom Literacy.* New York: Teachers College P, 1997. Print.

Engberg, Mark E. "Educating the Workforce for the 21st Century: A Cross-Disciplinary Analysis of the Impact of the Undergraduate Experience on Students' Development of a Pluralistic Orientation." *Research in Higher Education* 48.3 (2007): 283–317. Print.

———. "Improving Intergroup Relations in Higher Education: A Critical Examination of the Influence of Educational Interventions on Racial Bias." *Review of Educational Research* 74.4 (2004): 473–524. Print.

Etcoff, Nancy. *Survival of the Prettiest: The Science of Beauty.* New York: Anchor, 2000. Print.

Everts, Elisa. "Modalities of Turn-Taking in Blind/Sighted Interaction: Better to Be Seen and Not Heard?" *Discourse and Technology: Multimodal Discourse Analysis.* Ed. Philip LeVine and Ron Scollon. Washington, DC: Georgetown UP, 2004. 128–45. Print.

Fernheimer, Janice W. "Black Jewish Identity Conflict: A Divided Universal Audience and the Impact of Dissociative Disruption." *Rhetoric Society Quarterly* 39.1 (2009): 46–72. Print.

Fernsten, Linda. "Peer Response: Helpful Pedagogy or Hellish Event." *WAC Journal* 17 (2006): 33–41. Print.

Fisher v. University of Texas at Austin et al. 570 U.S. ___ (Citation 11-345). Supreme Court of the US. 2013. *LexisNexis Academic.* Web. 15 Jul 2013.

Fishman, Jenn, Andrea Lunsford, Beth McGregor, and Mark Otuteye. "Performing Writing, Performing Literacy." *College Composition and Communication* 57.2 (2005): 224–52. Print.

Fishman, Stephen M., and Lucille McCarthy. *Whose Goals, Whose Aspirations? Learning to Teach Underprepared Writers across the Curriculum.* Logan: Utah State UP, 2002. Print.

Flower, Linda. *Community Literacy and the Rhetoric of Public Engagement.* Carbondale: Southern Illinois UP, 2008. Print.

Flower, Linda, Elenore Long, and Lorraine Higgins. *Learning to Rival: A Literate Practice for Intercultural Inquiry.* Mahwah: Erlbaum, 2000. Print.

Fox, Helen. Afterword. *Social Change in Diverse Teaching Contexts: Touchy Subjects and Routine Practices.* Ed. Nancy G. Barron, Nancy M. Grimm, and Sibylle Gruber. New York: Lang, 2006. 251–66. Print.

Frankenberg, Ruth. *White Women, Race Matters: The Social Construction of Whiteness.* Minneapolis: U of Minnesota P, 1993. Print.

Frazier, Stefan. "Co-constructing Literacy Spaces: Examining the Talk of Undergraduate Composition Students in Classroom Peer Group Interaction." Diss. U of California Los Angeles, 2005. Print.

———. "Tellings of Remembrances 'Touched Off' by Student Reports in Group Work in Undergraduate Writing Classes." *Applied Linguistics* 28.2 (2007): 189–210. Print.

Freedman, Sarah Warshauer. "Outside-in and Inside-out: Peer Response Groups in Two Ninth-Grade Classes." *Research in the Teaching of English* 26.1 (1992): 71–107. Print.

French, Sally. "Simulation Exercises in Disability Awareness Training: A Critique." *Disability, Handicap and Society* 7.3 (1992): 257–66. Print.

Fulkerson, Richard. "The Toulmin Model of Argument and the Teaching of Composition." *Argument Revisited; Argument Redefined: Negotiating Meaning in the Composition Classroom.* Ed. Barbara Emmel, Paula Resch, and Deborah Tenney. Thousand Oaks: SAGE, 1996. 45–72. Print.

Fuller, David. "A Curious Case of Our Responding Habits: What Do We Respond to and Why?" *JAC* 8 (1988): 88–96. Print.

Gal, Susan. "Sociolinguistic Regimes and the Management of 'Diversity.'" *Language in Late Capitalism: Pride and Profit.* Ed. Alexandre Duchêne and Monica Heller. New York: Routledge, 2012. 22–42. Print.

Garfinkel, Harold. "The Origins of the Term 'Ethnomethodology.'" *Ethnomethodology.* Ed. Roy Turner. Harmondsworth: Penguin, 1974. 15–18. Print.

Gee, James Paul. *Social Linguistics and Literacies: Ideology in Discourses.* 4th ed. London: Routledge, 2012. Print.

Georgakopoulou, Alexandra. *Small Stories, Interaction, and Identities.* Amsterdam: Benjamins, 2007. Print.

———. "Styling Men and Masculinities: Interactional and Identity Aspects at Work." *Language in Society* 34.2 (2005): 163–84. Print.

———. "Thinking Big with Small Stories in Narrative and Identity Analysis." *Narrative Inquiry* 16.1 (2006): 122–30. Web. 21 Feb. 2009.

Gere, Anne Ruggles, and Robert D. Abbott. "Talking about Writing: The Language of Writing Groups." *Research in the Teaching of English* 19.4 (1985): 362–85. Print.

Gere, Anne Ruggles, and Ralph Stevens. "The Language of Writing Groups: How Oral Response Shapes Revision." *The Acquisition of Written Language*. Ed. Sarah Warshauer Freedman. Norwood: Ablex, 1985. 85–105. Print.

Gilyard, Keith, ed. *Race, Rhetoric, and Composition*. Portsmouth: Boynton/Cook, 1999. Print.

Giroux, Henry A. "Neoliberalism, Corporate Culture, and the Promise of Higher Education: The University as a Democratic Public Sphere." *Harvard Educational Review* 72.4 (2002): 425–63. Print.

Glazier, Jocelyn Anne. "Developing Cultural Fluency: Arab and Jewish Students Engaging in One Another's Company." *Harvard Educational Review* 73.2 (2003): 141–63. Print.

Glenn, Cheryl. *Unspoken: A Rhetoric of Silence*. Carbondale: Southern Illinois UP, 2004. Print.

Godbee, Beth. "Toward Explaining the Transformative Power of Talk about, around, and for Writing." *Research in the Teaching of English* 47.2 (2012): 171–97. Print.

Goodburn, Amy M. "Racing (Erasing) White Privilege in Teacher/Research Writing about Race." Gilyard 67–86.

Gomez, Mary Louise, Anne Burda Walker, and Michelle L. Page. "Personal Experience as a Guide to Teaching." *Teaching and Teacher Education* 16 (2000): 731–47. Print.

Gonçalves, Zan Meyer. *Sexuality and the Politics of Ethos*. Carbondale: Southern Illinois UP, 2005. Print.

Gonsalves, Lisa M. "Making Connections: Addressing the Pitfalls of White Faculty/Black Male Student Communication." *College Composition and Communication* 53.3 (2002): 435–65. Print.

González, Norma, Luis C. Moll, and Cathy Amanti, eds. *Funds of Knowledge: Theorizing Practices in Households, Communities, and Classrooms*. Mahwah: Erlbaum, 2005. Print.

Gratz v. Bollinger et al. 539 U.S. 244. Supreme Court of the US. 2003. *LexisNexis Academic*. Web. 15 Jun. 2010.

Greene, Stuart, and Erin Smith. "Teaching Talk about Writing: Student Conflict in Acquiring a New Discourse of Authorship through Collaborative Planning." *Teaching Academic Literacy: The Uses of Teacher-Research in Developing a Writing Program*. Ed. Katherine L. Weese, Stephen L. Fox, and Stuart Greene. Mahwah: Erlbaum, 1999. 149–74. Print.

Griffith, Jennifer R. "Writing Ethics: Person, Proximity, and Responsibility in a First-Year Composition Classroom." Diss. U of Wisconsin-Madison, 2006. Print.

Grutter v. Bollinger et al. 539 U.S. 306. Supreme Court of the US. 2003. *LexisNexis Academic.* Web. 15 Jun. 2010.

Gurin, Patricia, Eric L. Dey, Sylvia Hurtado, and Gerald Gurin. "Diversity and Higher Education: Theory and Impact on Educational Outcomes." *Harvard Educational Review* 72.3 (2002): 330–66. Print.

Halasek, Kay. *A Pedagogy of Possibility: Bakhtinian Perspectives on Composition Studies.* Carbondale: Southern Illinois UP, 1999. Print.

Hames-García, Michael. "What's at Stake in 'Gay' Identities?" Alcoff, et al. 78–95.

Harmon, Mary R. "Contact, Colonization, and Classrooms: Language Issues via Cisneros's *Woman Hollering Creek* and Villanueva's *Bootstraps.*" Wolff 197–212.

Harris, Joseph. "Negotiating the Contact Zone." *Journal of Basic Writing* 14.1 (1995): 27–42. Print.

Harvey, David. *A Brief History of Neoliberalism.* Oxford: Oxford UP, 2005. Print.

Haswell, Janis, and Richard Haswell. *Authoring: An Essay for the English Profession on Potentiality and Singularity.* Logan: Utah State UP, 2010. Print.

Haswell, Richard H. "NCTE/CCCC's Recent War on Scholarship." *Written Communication* 22.2 (2005): 198–223. Print.

Hawisher, Gail, and Cynthia L. Selfe, with Yi-Huey Guo, and Lu Liu. "Globalization and Agency: Designing and Redesigning the Literacies of Cyberspace." *College English* 68.6 (2006): 619–36. Print.

Heath, Shirley Brice. *Ways with Words: Language, Life, and Work in Communities and Classrooms.* Cambridge: Cambridge UP, 1983. Print.

Heilker, Paul, and Melanie Yergeau. "Autism and Rhetoric." *College English* 73.5 (2011): 485–97. Print.

Herrick, Jeanne Weiland. "Telling Stories: Rethinking the Personal Narrative in the Contact Zone of the Multicultural Classroom." Wolff 274–90.

Herrington, Anne, and Deborah Cadman. "Peer Review and Revising in an Anthropology Course: Lessons for Learning." *College Composition and Communication* 42.2 (1991): 184–99. Print.

Herrington, Anne J., and Marcia Curtis. *Persons in Process: Four Stories of Writing and Personal Development in College.* Urbana: NCTE, 2000. Print.

Hewett, Beth L. "Characteristics of Interactive Oral and Computer-Mediated Peer Group Talk and its Influence on Revision." *Computers and Composition* 17.3 (2000): 265–88. Print.

Hicks, Deborah. "Self and Other in Bakhtin's Early Philosophical Essays: Prelude to a Theory of Prose Consciousness." *Mind, Culture, and Activity* 7.3 (2000): 227–42. Print.

Hoang, Haivan V. "Campus Racial Politics and a 'Rhetoric of Injury.'" *College Composition and Communication* 61.1 (2009): W385-W408. *NCTE*. Web. 15 Jan. 2012.

hooks, bell. *Talking Back: Thinking Feminist, Thinking Black.* Boston: South End, 1989. Print.

Hull, Glynda, and Katherine Schultz, eds. *School's Out! Bridging Out-of-School Literacies with Classroom Practice.* New York: Teachers College P, 2002. Print.

Inkelas, Karen Kurotsuchi, and Matthew Soldner. "Undergraduate Living—Learning Programs and Student Outcomes." *Higher Education: Handbook of Theory Vol. 26.* Ed. John C. Smart and Michael B. Paulsen. New York: Springer, 2011. 1–55. Print.

Iverson, Susan V. "Constructing Outsiders: The Discursive Framing of Access in University Diversity Policies." *Review of Higher Education* 35.2 (2012): 149–77. Print.

Jayakumar, Uma M. "Can Higher Education Meet the Needs of an Increasingly Diverse and Global Society? Campus Diversity and Cross-Cultural Workforce Competencies." *Harvard Educational Review* 78.4 (2008): 615–51. Print.

Jung, Julie. *Revisionary Rhetoric, Feminist Pedagogy, and Multigenre Texts.* Carbondale: Southern Illinois UP, 2005. Print.

Jurecic, Ann. "Mindblindness: Autism, Writing, and the Problem of Empathy." *Literature and Medicine* 25.1 (2006): 1–23. *ProjectMuse.* Web. 26 Mar. 2012.

———. "Neurodiversity." *College English* 69.5 (2007): 421–42. Print.

Juzwik, Mary M. *The Rhetoric of Teaching: Understanding the Dynamics of Holocaust Narratives in an English Classroom.* Cresskill: Hampton, 2009. Print.

———. "Towards an Ethics of Answerability: Reconsidering Dialogism in Sociocultural Literacy Research." *College Composition and Communication* 55.3 (2004): 536–67. Print.

Juzwik, Mary M., Svjetlana Curcic, Kimberly Wolbers, Kathleen D. Moxley, Lisa M. Dimling, and Rebecca K. Shankland. "Writing Into the 21st Century: An Overview of Research on Writing, 1999 to 2004." *Written Communication* 23.4 (2006): 451–76. Print.

Juzwik, Mary M., and Denise Ives. "Small Stories as Resources for Performing Teacher Identity: Identity-in-Interaction in an Urban Language

Arts Classroom." *Narrative Inquiry* 20.1 (2010): 37–61. Web. 13 Apr. 2011.

Karabel, Jerome. *The Chosen: The Hidden History of Admission and Exclusion at Harvard, Yale, and Princeton.* Boston: Houghton, 2005. Print.

Kerschbaum, Stephanie L. "Classroom Narratives and Ethical Responsibility: How Markers of Difference Can Inform Teaching and Teacher Education." *Narrative Discourse Analysis for Teacher Educators: Managing Cultural Differences in Classrooms.* Ed. Lesley A. Rex and Mary M. Juzwik. Cresskill: Hampton, 2011. 77–104. Print.

———. "On Rhetorical Agency and Disclosing Disability in Academic Writing." *Rhetoric Review* 33.1 (forthcoming 2014).

Kuhne, Michael, and Gill Creel. "Student Evaluation and an Introduction to Academic Discourse: 'I Didn't Like it, and I Don't Know How to Improve it, Because it Works.'" *Teaching English in the Two-Year College* 33.3 (2006): 279–94. Print.

Labov, William. "The Transformation of Experience in Narrative Syntax." *Language in the Inner City: Studies in the Black English Vernacular.* By Labov. Philadelphia: U of Pennsylvania P, 1972. 354–96. Print.

Labov, William, and Joshua Waletzky. "Narrative Analysis: Oral Versions of Personal Experience." *Journal of Narrative and Life History* 7.1-4 (1997): 3–38. Print. Orig. pub. in *Essays on the Verbal and Visual Arts: Proceedings of the 1996 Annual Spring Meeting of the American Ethnological Society.* Ed. June Helm. Seattle: U of Washington P, 1967. 12–14.

LeCourt, Donna. *Identity Matters: Schooling the Student Body in Academic Discourse.* Albany: State U of New York P, 2004. Print.

———. "Performing Working-Class Identity in Composition: Toward a Pedagogy of Textual Practice." *College English* 69.1 (2006): 30–51. Print.

Lee, Amy. *Composing Critical Pedagogies: Teaching Writing as Revision.* Urbana: NCTE, 2000. Print.

Lemann, Nicholas. *The Big Test: The Secret History of the American Meritocracy.* New York: Farrar, 1999. Print.

Lemke, Jay L. "Across the Scales of Time: Artifacts, Activities, and Meanings in Ecosocial Systems." *Mind, Culture, and Activity* 7.4 (2000): 273–90. Web. 4 April 2011.

Levine, Arthur, and Jeanette S. Cureton. *When Hope and Fear Collide.* San Francisco: Jossey-Bass, 1998. Print.

Lewiecki-Wilson, Cynthia. "Teaching in the Contact Zone: Multiple Literacies/Deep Portfolio." Wolff 215–29.

Lewiecki-Wilson, Cynthia, and Brenda Jo Brueggemann, with Jay Dolmage. *Disability and the Teaching of Writing: A Critical Sourcebook.* Boston: Bedford/St. Martin's, 2008. Print.

Lewiecki-Wilson, Cynthia, Jay Dolmage, Paul Heilker, and Ann Jurecic. "Comment and Response: Two Comments on 'Neurodiversity.'" *College English* 70.3 (2008): 314–25. Print.

Lewis, Cynthia, Jean Ketter, and Bettina Fabos. "Reading Race in a Rural Context." *International Journal of Qualitative Studies in Education* 14.3 (2001): 317–50. Print.

Lieber, Andrea. "A Virtual *Veibershul:* Blogging and the Blurring of Public and Private among Orthodox Jewish Women." *College English* 72.6 (2010): 621–37. Print.

Lillis, Theresa. "Ethnography as Method, Methodology and 'Deep Theorizing': Closing the Gap between Text and Context in Academic Writing Research." *Written Communication* 25.3 (2008): 353–88. Print.

Lindquist, Julie. *A Place to Stand: Politics and Persuasion in a Working-Class Bar.* New York: Oxford UP, 2002. Print.

———. "What's the Trouble with Knowing Students? Only Time Will Tell." *Pedagogy* 10.1 (2010): 175–82. Web. 15 Jan. 2010.

Linton, Simi. *Claiming Disability: Knowledge and Identity.* New York: New York UP, 1998. Print.

Liu, Goodwin. "Affirmative Action in Higher Education: The Diversity Rationale and the Compelling Interest Test." *Harvard Civil Rights–Civil Liberties Law Review* 33 (1998): 381–442. *LexisNexis Academic.* Web. 8 Mar. 2012.

Lu, Min-Zhan. "From Silence to Words: Writing as Struggle." *College English* 49.4 (1987): 437–48. Print.

Lyons, Scott Richard. "Rhetorical Sovereignty: What Do American Indians Want from Writing?" *College Composition and Communication* 51.3 (2000): 447–68. Print.

Mathieu, Paula. "Economic Citizenship and the Rhetoric of Gourmet Coffee." *Rhetoric Review* 18.1 (1999): 112–27. Print.

McCall, Leslie. "The Complexity of Intersectionality." *Signs* 30.3 (2005): 1771–1800. Print.

Mehan, Hugh. *Learning Lessons: Social Organization in the Classroom.* Cambridge: Harvard UP, 1979. Print.

Michaels, Walter Benn. *The Trouble with Diversity: How We Learned to Love Identity and Ignore Inequality.* New York: Holt, 2006. Print.

Milem, Jeffrey F. "The Educational Benefits of Diversity: Evidence from Multiple Sectors." *Compelling Interest: Examining the Evidence on Racial*

Dynamics in Colleges and Universities. Ed. Mitchell J. Chang, Daria Witt, James Jones, and Kenji Hakuta. Stanford: Stanford UP, 2003. 126–69. Print.

Miller, D. Quentin. "The Trouble with the Other N-Word." *Chronicle of Higher Education* 29 Jul. 2012. Web. 29 Jul. 2012.

Miller, Richard E. "Fault Lines in the Contact Zone." *College English* 56.4 (1994): 389–409. Print.

Morris, Amanda Lynch. "Native American Stand-Up Comedy: Epideictic Strategies in the Contact Zone." *Rhetoric Review* 30.1 (2011): 37–53. Print.

Moya, Paula M. L. "What's Identity Got to Do with It? Mobilizing Identities in the Multicultural Classroom." Alcoff, et al. 96–117.

Moya, Paula M. L., and Michael R. Hames-García, eds. *Reclaiming Identity: Realist Theory and the Predicament of Postmodernism.* Berkeley: U of California P, 2000. Print.

Murray, Robert D. "Reconstitution and Race in the Contact Zone." Wolff 147–65.

Myers, Kristen. *Racetalk: Racism Hiding in Plain Sight.* Lanham: Rowman, 2005. Print.

Nathan, Rebekah. *My Freshman Year: What a Professor Learned by Becoming a Student.* New York: Penguin, 2005. Print.

Newfield, Christopher. *Unmaking the Public University: The Forty-Year Assault on the Middle Class.* Cambridge: Harvard UP, 2008. Print.

Nystrand, Martin. "Dialogic Discourse Analysis of Revision in Response Groups." *Discourse Studies in Composition.* Ed. Ellen Barton and Gail Stygall. Cresskill: Hampton, 2002. 377–92. Print.

———. "Learning to Write by Talking about Writing: A Summary of Research on Intensive Peer Review in Expository Writing Instruction at the University of Wisconsin-Madison." *The Structure of Written Communication: Studies in Reciprocity between Writers and Readers.* Ed. Martin Nystrand, with Margaret Himley, and Anne Doyle. Orlando: Academic, 1986. 179–211.

Nystrand, Martin, and Deborah Brandt. "Response to Writing as a Context for Learning to Write." *Writing and Response: Theory, Practice, and Research.* Ed. Chris M. Anson. Urbana: NCTE, 1989. 209–30. Print.

Nystrand, Martin, with Adam Gamoran, Robert Kachur, and Catherine Prendergast. *Opening Dialogue: Understanding the Dynamics of Language and Learning in the English Classroom.* New York: Teachers College P, 1997. Print.

O'Brien, Eileen. *Whites Confront Racism: Antiracists and Their Paths to Action.* Lanham: Rowman, 2001. Print.

Ochs, Elinor, and Lisa Capps. *Living Narrative: Creating Lives in Everyday Storytelling*. Cambridge: Harvard UP, 2001. Print.

Okawa, Gail Y. "'Resurfacing Roots': Developing a Pedagogy of Language Awareness from Two Views." *Language Diversity in the Classroom: From Intention to Practice*. Ed. Geneva Smitherman and Victor Villanueva. Carbondale: Southern Illinois UP, 2003. Print. 109–133.

Olson, Gary A. "Encountering the Other: Postcolonial Theory and Composition Scholarship." *Crossing Borderlands: Composition and Postcolonial Studies*. Ed. Andrea A. Lunsford and Lahoucine Ouzgane. Pittsburgh: U of Pittsburgh P, 2004. 84–94. Print.

Omi, Michael, and Howard Winant. *Racial Formation in the United States: From the 1960s to the 1990s*. 2nd ed. New York: Routledge, 1994. Print.

Ortiz, Anna M., and Silvia J. Santos. *Ethnicity in College: Advancing Theory and Improving Diversity Practices on Campus*. Sterling: Stylus, 2009. Print.

Ortmeier-Hooper, Christina. "English May Be My Second Language, But I'm Not 'ESL.'" *College Composition and Communication* 59.3 (2008): 389–419. Print.

Padilla, Raymond V., and Miguel Montiel. *Debatable Diversity: Critical Dialogues on Change in American Universities*. Lanham: Rowman, 1998. Print.

Patchan, Melissa M., Davida Charney, and Christian D. Schunn. "A Validation Study of Students' End Comments: Comparing Comments by Students, a Writing Instructor, and a Content Instructor." *Journal of Writing Research* 1.2 (2009): 124–52. Web. 13 Feb. 2012.

Patchan, Melissa M., Christian D. Schunn, and Russell J. Clark. "Writing in Natural Sciences: Understanding the Effects of Different Types of Reviewers on the Writing Process." *Journal of Writing Research* 2.3 (2011): 365–93. Web. 13 Feb. 2012.

Paulson, Eric J., Jonathan Alexander, and Sonya Armstrong. "Peer Review Re-Viewed: Investigating the Juxtaposition of Composition Students' Eye Movements and Peer-Review Processes." *Research in the Teaching of English* 41.3 (2007): 304–35. Print.

Penrose, Ann M. "Academic Literacy Perceptions and Performance: Comparing First-Generation and Continuing-Generation College Students." *Research in the Teaching of English* 36.4 (2002): 437–61. Print.

Pettigrew, Thomas F. "Intergroup Contact Theory." *Annual Review of Psychology* 49 (1998): 65–85. Print.

Pham, Vincent N., and Kent A. Ono, "'Artful Bigotry and Kitsch': A Study of Stereotype, Mimicry, and Satire in Asian American T-Shirt

Rhetoric." *Representations: Doing Asian American Rhetoric.* Ed. LuMing Mao and Morris Young. Logan: Utah State UP, 2008. 175–97. Print.

Pollock, Mica. *Colormute: Race Talk Dilemmas in an American School.* Princeton: Princeton UP, 2004. Print.

———, ed. *Everyday Antiracism: Getting Real About Race in School.* New York: New, 2008. Print.

Porter, Kevin J. "A Pedagogy of Charity: Donald Davidson and the Student-Negotiated Composition Classroom." *College Composition and Communication* 52.4 (2001): 574–611. Print.

Powell, Malea. "Blood and Scholarship: One Mixed-Blood's Story." Gilyard 1–16.

Powell, Pegeen Reichert. "Critical Discourse Analysis and Composition Studies: A Study of Presidential Discourse and Campus Discord." *College Composition and Communication* 55.3 (2004): 439–69. Print.

Pratt, Mary Louise. "Arts of the Contact Zone." *Profession* 91 (1991): 33–40. Print.

Prendergast, Catherine, and Nancy Abelmann. "Alma Mater: College, Kinship, and the Pursuit of Diversity." *Social Text* 24.1 (2006): 38–53. Print.

Price, Margaret. *Mad at School: Rhetorics of Mental Disability and Academic Life.* Ann Arbor: U of Michigan P, 2011. Print.

Purcell-Gates, Victoria. *Other People's Words: The Cycle of Low Literacy.* Cambridge: Harvard UP, 1995. Print.

Ratcliffe, Krista. *Rhetorical Listening: Identification, Gender, Whiteness.* Carbondale: Southern Illinois UP, 2005. Print.

Reda, Mary M. *Between Speaking and Silence: A Study of Quiet Students.* Albany: State U of New York P, 2009. Print.

Regents of the University of California v. Bakke. 438 U.S. 265. Supreme Court of the US. 1978. *LexisNexis Academic.* Web. 15 Jun. 2010.

Rex, Lesley A., and Mary M. Juzwik, eds. *Narrative Discourse Analysis for Teacher Educators: Managing Cultural Diversity in Classrooms.* Cresskill: Hampton, 2011. Print.

Rex, Lesley A., Timothy J. Murnen, Jack Hobbs, and David McEachen. "Teachers' Pedagogical Stories and the Shaping of Classroom Participation: 'The Dancer' and 'Graveyard Shift at the 7-11.'" *American Educational Research Journal* 39.3 (2002): 765–96. Print.

Ridgeway, Cecilia L. *Framed by Gender: How Gender Inequality Persists in the Modern World.* New York: Oxford UP, 2011. Print.

Rockquemore, Kerry Ann, and David L. Brunsma. *Beyond Black: Biracial Identity in America.* 2nd ed. Lanham: Rowman, 2008. Print.

Rodriguez, Richard. *Hunger of Memory: The Education of Richard Rodriguez.* New York: Bantam, 1982. Print.

Royster, Jacqueline Jones. *Traces of a Stream: Literacy and Social Change among African-American Women.* Pittsburgh: U of Pittsburgh P, 2000. Print.

———. "When the First Voice You Hear is Not Your Own." *College Composition and Communication* 47.1 (1996): 29–40. Print.

Rumsey, Suzanne Kesler. "Heritage Literacy: Adoption, Adaptation, and Alienation of Multimodal Literacy Tools." *College Composition and Communication* 60.3 (2009): 573–86. Print.

Sacks, Harvey, Emanuel A. Schegloff, and Gail Jefferson. "A Simplest Systematics for the Organization of Turn-Taking for Conversation." *Language* 50.4 (1974): 696–735. Print.

Sánchez, Rosaura. "On a Critical Realist Theory of Identity." Alcoff, et al. 31–52.

Sandel, Michael J. *What Money Can't Buy: The Moral Limits of Markets.* London: Allen Lane, 2012. Print.

Schiffrin, Deborah. "Everyday Argument: The Organization of Diversity in Talk." *Handbook of Discourse Analysis, vol. 3: Discourse and Dialogue.* Ed. Teun A. van Dijk. London: Academic, 1985. 35–46. Print.

Schroeder, Christopher. *Diverse by Design: Literacy Education within Multicultural Institutions.* Logan: Utah State UP, 2011. Print.

Schultz, Katherine. *Listening: A Framework for Teaching across Differences.* New York: Teachers College P, 2003. Print.

Scollon, Ron, and Suzanne B. K. Scollon. *Narrative, Literacy, and Face in Interethnic Communication.* Norwood: Ablex, 1981. Print.

Sidanius, Jim, Shana Levin, Colette van Laar, and David O. Sears. *The Diversity Challenge: Social Identity and Intergroup Relations on the College Campus.* New York: Russell Sage Foundation, 2008. Print.

Siebers, Tobin. "Disability in Theory: From Social Constructionism to the New Realism of the Body." *The Disability Studies Reader.* 2nd ed. Ed. Lennard J. Davis. New York: Routledge, 2006. 173–83. Print. Rpt. of "Disability in Theory: From Social Constructionism to Realism of the Body." *American Literary History* 13.4 (2001): 737–54.

———. *Disability Theory.* Ann Arbor: U of Michigan P, 2008. Print.

Silverstein, Michael. "Metapragmatic Discourse and Metapragmatic Function." *Reflexive Language: Reported Speech and Metapragmatics.* Ed. John A. Lucy. Cambridge: Cambridge UP, 1993. 33–58. Print.

Silverstein, Michael, and Greg Urban, eds. *Natural Histories of Discourse.* Chicago: U of Chicago P, 1996. Print.

Slaughter, Sheila, and Gary Rhoades. *Academic Capitalism and the New Economy: Markets, State, and Higher Education.* Baltimore: Johns Hopkins UP, 2004. Print.

Smith, Daryl G. *Diversity's Promise for Higher Education: Making it Work.* Baltimore: Johns Hopkins UP, 2009. Print.

Sohn, Kathleen Kelleher. "Whistlin' and Crowin' Women of Appalachia: Literacy Practices since College." *College Composition and Communication* 54.3 (2003): 423–52. Print.

Sommers, Elizabeth, and Sandra Lawrence. "Women's Ways of Talking in Teacher-Directed and Student-Directed Peer Response Groups." *Linguistics and Education* 4.1 (1992): 1–35. Print.

Spear, Karen. *Sharing Writing: Peer Response Groups in English Classes.* Portsmouth: Heinemann, 1988. Print.

Spigelman, Candace. "Habits of Mind: Historical Configurations of Textual Ownership in Peer Writing Groups. *College Composition and Communication* 49.2 (1998): 234–55. Print.

Steele, Claude M. *Whistling Vivaldi: How Stereotypes Affect Us and What We Can Do.* New York: Norton, 2010. Print.

Sternglass, Marilyn S. *Time to Know Them: A Longitudinal Study of Writing and Learning at the College Level.* Mahwah: Erlbaum, 1997. Print.

Stevens, Mitchell L. *Creating a Class: College Admissions and the Education of Elites.* Cambridge: Harvard UP, 2007. Print.

Stokoe, Elizabeth H., and Janet Smithson. "Making Gender Relevant: Conversation Analysis and Gender Categories in Interaction." *Discourse and Society* 12.2 (2001): 243–69. Print.

Strauss, Anselm, and Juliet Corbin. *Basics of Qualitative Research: Techniques and Procedures for Developing Grounded Theory.* 2nd ed. Thousand Oaks: SAGE, 1998. Print.

Sue, Derald Wing, Christina M. Capodilupo, Gina C. Torino, Jennifer M. Bucceri, Aisha M. B. Holder, Kevin L. Nadal, and Marta Esquilin. "Racial Microaggressions in Everyday Life: Implications for Clinical Practice." *American Psychologist* 62.4 (2007): 271–86. Print.

Sullivan, Patrick, and David Nielsen. "'Ability to Benefit': Making Forward-Looking Decisions about Our Most Underprepared Students." *College English* 75.3 (2013): 319–43. Print.

Takagi, Dana Y. *The Retreat from Race: Asian-American Admissions and Racial Politics.* New Brunswick: Rutgers UP, 1992. Print.

Tannen, Deborah. *You Just Don't Understand: Women and Men in Conversation.* New York: Morrow, 1990. Print.

———. *You're Wearing That?: Understanding Mothers and Daughters in Conversation.* New York: Random, 2006. Print.

Thompson, Isabelle. "Scaffolding in the Writing Center: A Microanalysis of an Experienced Tutor's Verbal and Nonverbal Tutoring Strategies." *Written Communication* 26.4 (2009): 417–53. Print.

Tinto, Vincent. *Leaving College: Rethinking the Causes and Cures of Student Attrition.* 2nd ed. Chicago: U of Chicago P, 1993. Print.

Tobin, Lad. *Writing Relationships: What* Really *Happens in the Composition Class.* Portsmouth: Boynton/Cook, 1993. Print.

Townsend, Jane S., and Danling Fu. "Quiet Students across Cultures and Contexts." *English Education* 31.1 (1998): 4–19. Print.

TuSmith, Bonnie, and Maureen Reddy, eds. *Race in the College Classroom: Pedagogy and Politics.* New Brunswick: Rutgers UP, 2002. Print.

Urciuoli, Bonnie. "Excellence, Leadership, Skills, Diversity: Marketing Liberal Arts Education." *Language and Communication* 23 (2003): 385–408. Print.

———. "Neoliberal Education: Preparing the Student for the New Workplace." *Ethnographies of Neoliberalism.* Ed. Carol J. Greenhouse. Philadelphia: U of Pennsylvania P, 2010. 162–76. Print.

———. "Skills and Selves in the New Workplace." *American Ethnologist* 35.2 (2008): 211–28. Print.

van Gennip, Nanine A. E., Mien S. R. Segers, and Harm H. Tillema. "Peer Assessment as a Collaborative Learning Activity: The Role of Interpersonal Variables and Conceptions." *Learning and Instruction* 20.4 (2010): 280–90. *ScienceDirect.* Web. 7 Mar. 2012.

van Slyck, Phyllis. "Repositioning Ourselves in the Contact Zone." *College English* 59.2 (1997): 149–70. Print.

Vidali, Amy. "Rhetorical Hiccups: Disability Disclosure in Letters of Recommendation." *Rhetoric Review* 28.2 (2009): 185–204. Print.

Villanueva, Victor, Jr. *Bootstraps: From an American Academic of Color.* Urbana: NCTE, 1993. Print.

Vuchinich, Samuel. "The Sequential Organization of Closing in Verbal Family Conflict." *Conflict Talk: Sociolinguistic Investigations of Arguments in Conversations.* Ed. Allen D. Grimshaw. Cambridge: Cambridge UP, 1990. 118–38. Print.

Wade, Lisa. "Doctoring Diversity: Race and Photoshop." *Sociological Images.* 2 Sept. 2009. Web. 27 Aug. 2010.

West, Candace, and Sarah Fenstermaker. "Accountability in Action: The Accomplishment of Gender, Race, and Class in a Meeting of the University of California Board of Regents." *Discourse and Society* 13.4 (2002): 537–63. Web. 13 May 2010.

Westbrook, Evelyn. "Community, Collaboration, and Conflict: The Community Writing Group as Contact Zone." *Writing Groups Inside and Outside the Classroom.* Ed. Beverly J. Moss, Nels P. Highberg, and Melissa Nicolas. Mahwah: Erlbaum, 2004. 229–48. Print.

Whitt, Elizabeth J., Marcia I. Edison, Ernest T. Pascarella, Patrick T. Terenzini, and Amaury Nora. "Influences on Students' Openness to Diversity and Challenge in the Second and Third Years of College." *Journal of Higher Education* 72.2 (2001): 172–204. Web. 15 Feb. 2012.

Williams, Kim M. *Mark One or More: Civil Rights in Multiracial America.* Ann Arbor: U of Michigan P, 2006. Print.

Winkle-Wagner, Rachelle. *The Unchosen Me: Race, Gender, and Identity among Black Women in College.* Baltimore: Johns Hopkins UP, 2009. Print.

Wolfe, Joanna. "Gesture and Collaborative Planning: A Case Study of a Student Writing Group." *Written Communication* 22.3 (2005): 298–332. Print.

Wolff, Janice M., ed. *Professing in the Contact Zone: Bringing Theory and Practice Together.* Urbana: NCTE, 2002. Print.

Wortham, Stanton. *Acting Out Participant Examples in the Classroom.* Philadelphia: Benjamins, 1994. Print.

———. "Interactional Positioning and Narrative Self-Construction." *Narrative Inquiry* 10.1 (2000): 157–84. Print.

———. *Learning Identity: The Joint Emergence of Social Identification and Academic Learning.* New York: Cambridge UP, 2006. Print.

———. *Narratives in Action: A Strategy for Research and Analysis.* New York: Teachers College P, 2001. Print.

Yanow, Dvora. *Constructing 'Race' and 'Ethnicity' in America: Category-Making in Public Policy and Administration.* Armonk: Sharpe, 2003. Print.

Young, Morris. *Minor Re/Visions: Asian American Literacy Narratives as a Rhetoric of Citizenship.* Carbondale: Southern Illinois UP, 2004. Print.

DIVERSITY DOCUMENTS FROM MIDWESTERN UNIVERSITY

"Annual Data Release." PowerPoint presentation. 2004–2005. Web. 30 Jun. 2010.

"Annual Data Release." PowerPoint presentation. 2011–2012. Web. 2 Jul. 2012.

"Application for Undergraduate Admission." PDF document. 2003–2004. Email. 3 Jul. 2012.

"Application for Undergraduate Admission." PDF document. 2011–2012. Web. 25 Jun. 2012.

"Diversity in Admissions." Web site. Web. 27 June 2012.

"Diversity Report." PowerPoint presentation. Sept. 2011. Web. 25 Jun. 2012.

"Information for Users of Student Race/Ethnicity Data at [Midwestern University]." Microsoft Word document. Sept. 2009. Web. 6 Mar. 2010.

Midwestern University Diversity Agenda. 1998. Print.

"Office for Diversity." Web. 1 Aug. 2012.

"Provost's Statement on Diversity." Web. 4 Jul. 2012.

"To the [Midwestern] Community." 2009. Web. 6 Mar. 2010.

"Updated Diversity Plan." 2011. Web. 27 June 2012.

INDEX

Abbott, R. D., 157
Abelmann, N., 37, 38
Admission policies, 37
Affirmative action, rationale for, 33
Ahmed, S., 29, 152
Alcoff, L. M., 83, 90, 111, 156
Alexander, J., 5, 86, 87, 157
Allport, G. W., 82
Amanti, C., 155
Answerability, 76–77, 134, 148
Armstrong, S., 86, 87, 157
Astin, A., 84, 136
Autism, 59–62, 63–64

Bakhtin, M., 26, 65, 67–71, 76, 77, 134
Bamberg, M., 23, 102, 107
Baumann, R., 76
Beaufort, A., 56
Beauvais, B. J., 82
Bell, J., 45
Bialostosky, D. H., 76, 78
Blommaert, J., 30, 31
Bonilla-Silva, E., 17
Bordo, S., 94
Brandt, D., 157
Brayboy, B. M. J., 3, 9, 10
Brewer, E., 153
Brooke, R., 157
Brown, K., 46
Brown, N., 98
Brown, S. G., 13
Brueggemann, B. J., 6, 155
Brunsma, D., 43

Bucceri, J. M., 135
Burgess, A., 13

Cadman, D., 157
Campbell, M. E., 156
Canagarajah, A. S., 82
Capodilupo, C. M., 135
Capps, L., 90
Carroll, L. A., 56
Carter, S., 88
Categorical redefinition of difference, 10–12
Cazden, C. B., 157
Chang, M. J., 46
Charney, D., 157
Cheryan, S., 156
Cheu, J., 6
Ching, K. L., 157
Chiseri-Strater, E., 2
Cho, K., 157
Christoph, J. N., 89
Classroom discourse, 22–23, 29
  institutional context for, 29
  recording and transcribing, 22–23
Classroom participation, 1, 2–3, 88–89
Cole, D., 82
Conflict. See Disagreement
Contact zones, 16, 79–89
  classroom as, 83–89
  research on, 82
Contextualization, 23
Corbin, J., 23
Corporate discourse, 29

Crable, B., 29
Craig, C. L., 13, 151
Creel, G., 86
Crenshaw, K. W., 10
Critical discourse analysis, 24, 26, 29–30
Cultural groups, framing of, 3–4
Curcic, S., 13
Cureton, J. S., 84, 136
Curry, T. J., 120
Curtis, M., 2, 13, 56
Cushman, E., 5

Danis, M. F., 157
Data analysis, 21–24
Data generation, 21
David, D., 157
De, E. N., 8, 9, 10, 153
Deafness, 65–66, 156
DeFina, A., 17, 156
Delpit, L., 58
Denson, N., 46
Determinant factors, 8
Dey, E. L., 46, 84
Dialogic discourse analysis, 23
Dialogism, 16, 76
Difference. *See also* Diversity
   avoiding, 135–49
   awareness of, 6
   categorical redefinition of, 10–12
   engagement with, 15–25, 75–78, 83–89
   fixing, 6, 12–15, 59–64
   identification of, 13
   listening to, 66
   markers of, 70–73
   marking. *See* Marking difference
   as property, 25, 26, 57–78
   as relation between individuals, 67
   research on, 5, 7–15
   versus sameness, 136–37
   taxonomizing, 7–10
Dimling, L. M., 13
Disability, 59–62, 63–64

Disagreement, 82–83, 89–90, 93–101, 119–35
   peer review example of, 93–101, 119–35
   stalemate in, 131–35
Diversity. *See also* Difference
   definitions of, 30, 32, 44–47
   discourse on, 29, 47–55
   interactional, 84
   mainstream view of, 45
   market for, in higher education, 32–39
   versus multiculturalism, 45
   as property, 25, 26, 32, 39–44
   structural, 46, 79
Diversity discourse, 29, 33, 37–45
   market values in, 33
Dobrin, S. I., 13
Dolmage, J., 64, 66
Dorner, R., 61
Dryer, D. B., 9
Duffy, J., 55, 57, 61
Dunn, P. A., 5, 6
Duranti, A., 23
Dynamism, 26, 57, 67, 68–69
Dyson, A. H., 16

Edison, M. I., 84, 136
Educational background, 8
Emergence, 26, 57, 70
Engagement, 15–25, 75–78, 116–17, 134, 148
   answerable, 76–78, 134, 148
   motivation for, 15, 83–89
   role of writing in, 16
   study of, 15–18
Engberg, M. E., 36, 82
English as a Second Language (ESL), limitations of label, 11–12
Esquilin, M., 135
Etcoff, N., 94
Ethnicity. *See* Race and ethnicity
Ethnographic research, 1–2, 13
Evans, R., 157

Everts, E., 158

Fabos, B., 6
Fenstermaker, S., 17, 156
Fernheimer, J. W., 5
Fernstein, L., 157
Fishman, J., 56
Fishman, S. M., 2, 56
Fixing difference, 6, 12–15, 59–64
Flower, L., 5, 76
Fox, H., 3
Frankenberg, R., 72
Frazier, S., 157
Freedman, S. W., 86, 87, 157
French, S., 61
Fu, D., 2
Fulkerson, R., 85
Fuller, D., 100

Gal, S., 154
Garfinkel, H., 19
Gee, J. P., 23, 30, 31
Gender, 73
Gender inequality, 14
Generalizations, avoiding, 113–15
Georgakopoulou, A., 23, 102
Gere, A. R., 157
Giroux, H., 33
Glazier, J., 131
Glenn, C., 3
Godbee, B., 88, 158
Gomez, M. L., 61
Gonçalves, Z. M., 13
Gonsalves, L., 62
González, N., 155
Goodburn, A. M., 158
Goodwin, C., 23
Greene, S., 157
Gregory, D. U., 8, 9, 10, 153
Griffith, J. R., 87, 157
Grounded theory, 23
Grutter v. Bollinger et al., 33
Gurin, G., 46, 84
Gurin, P., 46, 79, 84

Halasek, K., 16, 76
Hames-García, M., 64, 156
Harmon, M. R., 82
Harris, J., 80, 81, 82, 154
Hartmann, D., 45
Harvey, D., 35
Haswell, J., 14
Haswell, R. H., 14, 157
Hawisher, G., 13
Heath, S. B., 57
Heifferon, B. A., 6
Heilker, P., 63, 64, 66
Herrick, J. W., 82
Herrington, A. J., 2, 13, 56, 157
Hewett, B. L., 157
Hicks, D., 76
Higgins, L., 5
Higher education, 29, 32–39, 150–52
    affirmative action in, 33
    corporate culture in, 33
    diversity policies in, 150
    institutional discourse in, 29, 150
    market for diversity in, 32–39
Hoang, H. V., 18, 55, 112, 154
Hobbs, J., 114
Holder, A. M. B., 135
hooks, b., 4, 88
Hull, G., 57
Hurtado, S., 46, 84

Identifiers, use in classroom, 17
Identity categories, 4, 5, 7–9, 64–66,
    73–74, 153–54
    contextualization of, 5
    determinant factors of, 8
    interrelationships among, 7–9
    limitations, 64
    renaming, 153–54
Identity construction, 18, 90, 91
Identity contingencies, 9, 93
Indexicality, 23
Inkelas, K. K., 154
Institutional discourse, 29, 150
Interactional diversity, 84

Intersectional analysis, 10, 64
Ivanič, R., 13
Iverson, S., 150, 152
Ives, D., 93, 114

Jayakumar, U., 34, 36
Jefferson, G., 23
Jung, J., 13
Jurecic, A., 59–62, 63–64, 66, 75
Juzwik, M. M., 13, 93, 113, 114, 157

Karabel, J., 32
Kerschbaum, S. L., 24, 106
Ketter, J., 6
Kuhne, M., 86

Labov, W., 90, 102, 107
Lawrence, S., 157
LeCourt, D., 5, 14, 88
Lee, A., 13
Lemann, N., 32
Lemke, J. L., 13
Levin, S., 85
Levine, A., 84, 136
Lewiecki-Wilson, C., 6, 64, 66, 82, 155
Lewis, C., 6
Lieber, A., 5
Lillis, T., 13
Lindquist, J., 56, 89
Linton, S., 153
Listening, 13, 66
Liu, G., 34
Long, E., 5
López, S., 156
Lu, M. Z., 88
Lunsford, A., 56

MacArthur, C., 157
Markers of difference, 70–73, 75
Marking difference, 6–7, 26–27, 57–59, 62, 64, 73–74, 83, 89–117, 118, 135
    coming-to-know students and, 57–59

as constant process, 74
difficulties of, 118, 135
identity categories and, 73–74
implications for teaching, 112–17
intersectionality and, 64
limitations of, 27, 118
opportunities for rhetorical action through, 115–16
in peer review, 89–112
resources for, 62
teacher awareness of, 112
Mathieu, P., 29
McCall, L., 10
McCarthy, L., 2, 56
McEachen, D., 114
McGregor, B., 56
McKinley, B., 2
Mehan, H., 157
Michaels, W. B., 36
Midwestern University Diversity Agenda (MUDA), 31, 34–39, 47–55, 155
    definition of diversity in, 44
    goals of, 51
    market values in, 34–39
    rationale for, 34
    targeted ethnic groups in, 37, 45–46, 47
    use of pronouns in, 47–52, 155
    who's who in, 47–55
Milem, J. F., 46
Miller, D., 43
Miller, R., 82
Mirtz, R., 157
Misa, K., 46
Mohanty, S. P., 156
Moll, L. C., 155
Monin, B., 156
Montiel, M., 32
Morris, A. L., 5
Moxley, K. D., 13
Moya, P., 15, 156
Multicultural bazaar, 80, 146, 154
Multiculturalism, versus diversity, 45
Murnen, T. J., 114

Murray, R. D., 82
Myers, K., 17
MyRichUncle website, 38

Nadal, K. L., 135
Narratives, 82–83, 89, 90, 101–12
   definition of, 90, 102
   peer review example of, 101–12
Nathan, R., 84, 136
Neoliberalism, 35
Newfield, C., 37
Nora, A., 84, 136
Nielsen, D., 4, 75
Nystrand, M., 16, 23, 89, 157

O'Brien, E., 88
Ochs, E., 90
O'Connor, S. D., 33
Okawa, G. Y., 4
Olson, G., 80, 82
Omi, M., 73
Ono, K. A., 156
Ortiz, A. M., 42
Ortmeier-Hooper, C., 11, 12
Otherness, confrontation with, 80
Otuteye, M., 56
Overidentification, 14

Padilla, R. V., 32
Page, M. L., 61
Participation in classroom, 1, 2,
   88–89
Pascarella, E. T., 84, 136
Patchan, M. M., 157
Paulson, E. J., 86, 87, 157
Peer review, 18, 23–24, 86–112,
   119–49, 157
   articulating authority in, 97, 101
   avoiding difference in, 135–49
   competing textual meanings in,
      119–35
   confrontation in, 86–89
   dialogic discourse analysis of, 23–24
   disagreement during, 82–83,
      89–90, 93–101

identity construction during, 18
limitations of marking difference
   in, 119–35
marking difference in, 86–87,
   89–112
narrative in, 82–83, 89, 90, 101–12
personal nature of, 132–35
power dynamics in, 99–100
research on, 157
structure of, 90
student comments in, 138
Penrose, A. M., 40
Perryman-Clark, S. M., 13, 151
Pettigrew, T. F., 88
Pham, V. N., 156
Physical appearance, 98
Pollock, M., 6, 17, 58, 112
Porter, K., 86
Positioning, 23
Powell, M., 13
Powell, P., 18, 29
Power asymmetries, 10
Pratt, M. L., 16, 79, 80, 81
Prendergast, C., 37, 38
Price, M., 3, 60, 155
Pronouns, in Midwestern University
   Diversity Agenda, 47–52
Purcell-Gates, V., 5, 57

Race and ethnicity, 8, 17–18, 39–43,
   45–46, 73
   categorization of, 39–43
   focus on, in MUDA, 45–46
   public dialogue about, 17–18
Ratcliffe, K., 13, 58, 66, 113, 119
Reda, M., 2
Reddy, M., 58, 62
Reflexivity, 4
Relationality, 26, 57, 69, 71
Research, 1–3, 5–6, 7–15, 18–25,
   56–57, 157
   audience for, 25
   classroom application of, 5–6,
      13–14
   on classroom participation, 2–3

on contact zones, 82
data analysis for, 21–24
data generation for, 21
on difference and diversity, 5, 7–15
ethnographic, 1–2, 13
intersectional analysis, 10
longitudinal, 56–57
participants in, 18–21
on peer review, 157
study design and implementation,
    18–25
Rex, L., 114
Rhoades, G., 36
Ridgeway, C., 13–14, 73
Rockquemore, K. A., 43
Rodriguez, R., 88
Roommate assignments, 85
Royster, J. J., 5, 13
Rumsey, S., 13

Sacks, H., 23
Sáenz, V., 46
Sánchez, R., 4
Sandel, M. J., 32, 33, 35, 46
Santos, S. J., 42
Schegloff, E. A., 23
Schiffrin, D., 90
Schroeder, C., 9, 29, 36, 41, 156
Schultz, K., 57, 58
Schunn, C. D., 157
Scollon, R., 23
Scollon, S. B. K., 23
Sears, D. O., 85
Second language students, 11–12
Selfe, C., 13
Self-identifications, perception and,
    10
Shankland, R. K., 13
Sidanius, J., 85
Siebers, T., 154
Silence, in classroom, 3
Silverstein, M., 23, 127
Situatedness, 13
Slaughter, S., 36

Smith, D. G., 46
Smith, E., 157
Smithson, J., 148
Sohn, K. K., 5
Soldner, M., 154
Sommers, E., 157
Spear, K., 86, 132, 136, 157
Spigelman, C., 157
Steele, C., 9
Stereotypes, avoiding, 2
Sternglass, M. S., 56
Stevens, M. L., 54
Stevens, R., 157
Stokoe, E., 148
Storytelling, 114–15
Strauss, A., 23
Structural diversity, 46, 79
Students, 1, 2–3, 11–12, 39, 54,
    56–57, 66, 74–75, 84, 118–19,
    136, 150
  anxiety of, about writing, 118–19
  coming-to-know, 56–57
  as implementer of diversity, 54
  intergroup interactions among,
    84–85
  learning with, 57, 66, 74–75
  marketability of, 39
  minority, 150
  second language, 11–12
  self-segregation impulse of, 84, 136
  participation of, 1, 2–3
  recruiting of, 55
Sue, D. W., 135
Sullivan, P., 4, 75

Takagi, D. Y., 32
Tannen, D., 158
Taxonomizing difference, 7–10
Teachers, 14, 112
  awareness of marking difference,
    112
  positioning of, 14
Teacher–student relationships, 1–2,
    56–57

establishing, 56–57

Terenzini, P. T., 84, 136

Textual meanings, competing versions of, 119–35

Thompson, I., 158

Tillema, H. H., 157

Tinto, V., 40

Tobin, L., 86

Torino, G. C., 135

Toulmin, S., 20, 85

Townsend, J., 2

Transcripts of classroom discourse, analyzing, 22–23

Troyer, L., 156

TuSmith, B., 58, 62

Urban, G., 23

Urciuoli, B., 36, 45

van Gennip, N. A. E., 157

van Laar, C., 85

van Slyck, P., 8

Verb aspect, 129–31

Verschueren, J., 30, 31

Vidali, A., 61

Villanueva, V., 4, 88

Visible identities, 90, 111

Vuchinich, S., 90, 97

Wade, L., 39

Waletszky, J., 90, 107

Walker, A. B., 61

West, C., 17, 156

Westbrook, E., 157

White, L. F., 6

Whiteness, 13, 72

Whitt, E. J., 84, 136

Williams, K. M., 43

Winant, H., 73

Winkle-Wagner, R., 58, 137

Wolbers, K., 13

Wolfe, J., 158

Wolff, J., 16

Wortham, S., 13, 23, 112, 114, 127, 157

Writing, 16, 118–19

anxiety about, 118–19

role in engagement with difference, 16

Yanow, D., 40, 42, 43

Yergeau, M., 63, 64

Young, M., 4, 13

AUTHOR

Stephanie L. Kerschbaum is assistant professor of English at the University of Delaware. She has published essays in *College Composition and Communication*, *Academe*, *Profession*, *Rhetoric Review*, *Kairos*, and two edited collections.

OTHER BOOKS IN THE CCCC STUDIES IN WRITING & RHETORIC SERIES

Toward a New Rhetoric of Difference
Stephanie L. Kerschbaum

Rhetoric of Respect: Recognizing Change at a Community Writing Center
Tiffany Rousculp

After Pedagogy: The Experience of Teaching
Paul Lynch

Redesigning Composition for Multilingual Realities
Jay Jordan

Agency in the Age of Peer Production
Quentin D. Vieregge, Kyle D. Stedman, Taylor Joy Mitchell, and Joseph M. Moxley

Remixing Composition: A History of Multimodal Writing Pedagogy
Jason Palmeri

First Semester: Graduate Students, Teaching Writing, and the Challenge of Middle Ground
Jessica Restaino

Agents of Integration: Understanding Transfer as a Rhetorical Act
Rebecca S. Nowacek

Digital Griots: African American Rhetoric in a Multimedia Age
Adam J. Banks

The Managerial Unconscious in the History of Composition Studies
Donna Strickland

Everyday Genres: Writing Assignments across the Disciplines
Mary Soliday

The Community College Writer: Exceeding Expectations
Howard Tinberg and Jean-Paul Nadeau

A Taste for Language: Literacy, Class, and English Studies
James Ray Watkins

Before Shaughnessy: Basic Writing at Yale and Harvard, 1920–1960
Kelly Ritter

Writer's Block: The Cognitive Dimension
Mike Rose

Teaching/Writing in Thirdspaces: The Studio Approach
Rhonda C. Grego and Nancy S. Thompson

Rural Literacies
Kim Donehower, Charlotte Hogg, and Eileen E. Schell

Writing with Authority: Students' Roles as Writers in Cross-National Perspective
David Foster

Whistlin' and Crowin' Women of Appalachia: Literacy Practices since College
Katherine Kelleher Sohn

Sexuality and the Politics of Ethos in the Writing Classroom
Zan Meyer Gonçalves

African American Literacies Unleashed: Vernacular English and the Composition Classroom
Arnetha F. Ball and Ted Lardner

Revisionary Rhetoric, Feminist Pedagogy, and Multigenre Texts
Julie Jung

Archives of Instruction: Nineteenth-Century Rhetorics, Readers, and Composition Books in the United States
Jean Ferguson Carr, Stephen L. Carr, and Lucille M. Schultz

Response to Reform: Composition and the
Professionalization of Teaching
Margaret J. Marshall

Multiliteracies for a Digital Age
Stuart A. Selber

Personally Speaking: Experience as Evidence
in Academic Discourse
Candace Spigelman

Self-Development and College Writing
Nick Tingle

Minor Re/Visions: Asian American Literacy
Narratives as a Rhetoric of Citizenship
Morris Young

A Communion of Friendship: Literacy,
Spiritual Practice, and Women in Recovery
Beth Daniell

Embodied Literacies: Imageword and a
Poetics of Teaching
Kristie S. Fleckenstein

Language Diversity in the Classroom: From
Intention to Practice
edited by Geneva Smitherman and Victor
Villanueva

Rehearsing New Roles: How College Students
Develop as Writers
Lee Ann Carroll

Across Property Lines: Textual Ownership in
Writing Groups
Candace Spigelman

Mutuality in the Rhetoric and Composition
Classroom
David L. Wallace and Helen Rothschild
Ewald

The Young Composers: Composition's
Beginnings in Nineteenth-Century Schools
Lucille M. Schultz

Technology and Literacy in the Twenty-
First Century: The Importance of Paying
Attention
Cynthia L. Selfe

Women Writing the Academy: Audience,
Authority, and Transformation
Gesa E. Kirsch

Gender Influences: Reading Student Texts
Donnalee Rubin

Something Old, Something New: College
Writing Teachers and Classroom Change
Wendy Bishop

Dialogue, Dialectic, and Conversation: A
Social Perspective on the Function of Writing
Gregory Clark

Audience Expectations and Teacher Demands
Robert Brooke and John Hendricks

Toward a Grammar of Passages
Richard M. Coe

Rhetoric and Reality: Writing Instruction in
American Colleges, 1900–1985
James A. Berlin

Writing Groups: History, Theory, and
Implications
Anne Ruggles Gere

Teaching Writing as a Second Language
Alice S. Horning

Invention as a Social Act
Karen Burke LeFevre

The Variables of Composition: Process and
Product in a Business Setting
Glenn J. Broadhead and Richard C. Freed

Writing Instruction in Nineteenth-Century
American Colleges
James A. Berlin

*Computers & Composing: How the New
Technologies Are Changing Writing*
Jeanne W. Halpern and Sarah Liggett

*A New Perspective on Cohesion in Expository
Paragraphs*
Robin Bell Markels

Evaluating College Writing Programs
Stephen P. Witte and Lester Faigley

This book was typeset in Garamond and Frutiger by Barbara Frazier.
Typefaces used on the cover include Adobe Garamond and Formata.
The book was printed on 55-lb. Natural Offset paper
by Versa Press, Inc.